AMERICAN HABITS—AMUSING, INTERESTING . . . AND WEIRD!

* 18% twist their Oreos apart before eating them.

* Over 49% sleep with two pillows; 10% with three!

* 27% of teeth brushers use a circular motion.

* 57% reuse giftwrap; 54% regift an unwanted present for someone else.

* Three out of every ten can lift one eyebrow at a time.

* Three out of four first-time brides wear an engagement ring (average value: $1,597).

* 28% haven't filed a tax return in any given year.

* For $10 million, one quarter would abandon all their friends, and their church, become a hooker, or even undergo a race or sex change!

"*Are You Normal?* is the ultimate reality check."

— *~~nde*

EXCERPTED IN *LADIES' HOME JOURN*

ARE YOU NORMAL?

BERNICE KANNER

ST. MARTIN'S PAPERBACKS

Printed in the United States of America

St. Martin's Paperbacks trade paperback edition/September 1995

10 9 8 7 6 5 4 3 2 1

TABLE OF CONTENTS

INTRODUCTION:
ARE YOU NORMAL?

Most of us, on average, swear 16 times a day. (Those with kids seem to do it less.) Cut them off on the highway and more than half the drivers in America will do absolutely *nothing*. Most of us place the return address on an envelope on the front left corner, avoiding the back flap as if it were Zaire. And almost all of us feel strongly—one way or another—on how to hang the toilet paper: whether it should come off the roll from the top or underneath.

How do you fit in? In other words . . . are you "normal?" Do you conform to a type, standard, or pattern the way *most* Americans do?

I've spent the last two years asking Americans how they do it—how they wash their hair, floss their teeth, make the bed and get into it, apply makeup, and make up with each other. I haven't asked them how they feel about Whitewater or abortion, however, because every standard research survey has done that—and because I find it less interesting than the peculiarities of our behavior.

Instead, I've focused on stuff I consider important—such as what bathroom stall you'd select and how you deal with toilet tissue, and whether you save rubber bands or reuse gift wrap, and what position you sleep in.

Some giant ad agencies and research houses helped me. Leo Burnett, the Chicago-based home of the Keebler Elves, tough-talking Charlie the Starkist Tuna, the Jolly Green Giant, the lonely Maytag repairman, and that finicky feline Morris did my first foray which resulted in articles on the Examined Life in *New York Magazine* and *Reader's Digest* and dozens of media interviews. Then McCann-Erickson, whose megaclients include Exxon, Coca-Cola, AT&T, RJR Nabisco, American Home Products, and General Motors. McCann enlisted CMR Market Research in New York to field many questions nationwide.

"It's amazing how many people will let you look into their medicine cabinets, eavesdrop on their voicemail, and tell you things they don't even tell their mates," says Gary Soloshatz, president of CMR.

"In these true confessions people aren't telling us how they think they should feel; they're telling us how they do feel and how they do things that no one else ever asked," says Stacey Lesser, director of McCann-Erickson's strategic planning department. "There's nothing politically correct here. When people are willing to open their bathroom door while peeing, they're showing us that they're a lot more regular than we thought. Maybe they don't offend so easily. Maybe they're more relaxed than we assumed."

In some ways, we Americans are entirely predictable; in others we're puzzlingly iconoclastic. In still others, we're just downright surprising. Who'd have guessed that three of every four have made no "pre-need" burial arrangements, that in this age of neurosis only 14 percent of us have ever attended a self-help session, that a third of us do our Christmas shopping virtually year round, but that 22 percent of men and 9 percent of women leave it for the day or two before, and that by and large, we can't swallow pills without water?

See how you compare. Answers will come at the end of the book.

1) **DO YOU**
   a) reach behind the first milk in the dairy case for a fresher one?
   b) use the slit in your underwear (men)?
   c) eat corn on the cob methodically, row by row?

d) place the return address on the front left corner of an envelope?

e) keep both hands on the wheel when driving?

f) squeeze the toothpaste tube from the middle?

2) **WHEN YOU DON'T WANT SOMETHING IN YOUR SHOPPING CART DO YOU**

a) leave it in another part of the store wherever you are when you realize you don't want it?

b) hide it behind something else?

c) take it back to its rightful place?

d) ask a stock clerk to replace it?

e) leave it at the checkout counter?

3) **WOULD YOU EVER**

a) water down the liquor to accommodate more guests?

b) pour generic products into brand name containers?

c) do your children's homework for them instead of guiding them?

d) ask a doctor to fudge a diagnosis so insurance picks up the whole bill?

e) take supplies from work for home use?

4) **HOW DO YOU OPEN THE MAIL?**

a) With a letter opener.

b) Rip across the top.

c) Neatly tear the flap.

d) Rip off one end.

5) **WHICH DO YOU EAT FIRST,**

a) the frosting?

b) the cake?

c) both together?

6) **DO YOU EAT AN OREO**

a) whole and pure?

b) twisted apart?

c) dunked?

d) doctored with ice cream or other accompaniment?
e) smashed?

7) IN WHAT ORDER DO YOU DRESS?
a) Undies, bra, pantyhose.
b) Bra, undies, pantyhose.
c) Pantyhose, undies, bra.
d) Bra, pantyhose, undies.
e) Undies, pantyhose, bra.
f) Pantyhose, bra, undies.
g) Can't recall or don't want to.

8) HOW MANY PILLOWS DO YOU USUALLY SLEEP WITH?
a) None.
b) One.
c) Two.
d) Three.
e) Four or more.

9) IN THE JOHN DO YOU
a) insert the toilet paper so it will be pulled from over the top?
b) always put down the seat after you've peed?
c) sit on public toilets?
d) choose the handicapped stall over all other equal choices?
e) turn on the water to disguise the sound of pee?

10) HAVE YOU EVER
a) been bumped by an airline?
b) run out of gas?
c) skinny-dipped with the opposite sex?
d) sunbathed nude?
e) had a professional massage?

11) DO YOU
a) request the window seat on an airplane?
b) keep both hands on the wheel when you drive?

c) speed up at yellow lights?
d) floss?
e) bite your nails?
f) usually pick off your scabs?

12) IF ANOTHER DRIVER CUT YOU OFF SHARPLY WOULD YOU
a) let it slide and do nothing?
b) yell an obscenity?
c) give them the finger?
d) shake your fists or gesticulate?
e) flash your lights?
f) tailgate?
g) do something else—pull a gun, cut them off or turn them in on the car phone?

13) DO YOU BRUSH YOUR TEETH
a) up and down?
b) in a fastidious circular motion?
c) side to side?
d) angled?
e) electrically?
f) let them soak?

14) CAN YOU
a) cross your eyes?
b) flare your nostrils?
c) snap your fingers?
d) whistle loudly?
e) roll your tongue?
f) wiggle your ears?
g) raise one eyebrow at a time?
h) juggle?
i) do a split?

15) AS FOR ANNOYING HABITS, DO YOU
a) tap or jiggle your knees or legs?
b) chew on ice?

    c) crack your knuckles?
    d) regularly chew a pen cap or pencil?
    e) peel the labels off bottles or cans?
    f) twist or pull on your hair?
    g) twist the phone cord?
    h) grind your teeth?

16) IN A RESTAURANT DO YOU EVER
    a) send food back?
    b) take home leftovers?
    c) stiff the waiter for poor service?
    d) ask to change tables?
    e) ask another patron not to smoke?

17) DO YOU SET YOUR WATCH AHEAD?
    a) Why should I?
    b) Yeah, five minutes.
    c) Yeah, 10 minutes.
    d) Yeah, but I don't know how much.
    e) Don't wear a watch.

18) WHEN IT COMES TO BOOKS DO YOU SOMETIMES
    a) read the last page first—or otherwise skip ahead?
    b) always finish a book once you start it?
    c) fold down the page to use as a bookmark?

19) WHEN IT COMES TO HOUSEHOLD MANAGEMENT DO YOU
    a) make the bed daily?
    b) alphabetize your books?
    c) wear rubber gloves to clean?

20) DO YOU SAVE AND RECYCLE
    a) tinfoil?
    b) rubber bands?
    c) wrapping paper?
    d) gifts given to you that you don't want?
    e) old pennies?

Our Body Ills and Skills

DO YOU HAVE SOME ANNOYING NERVOUS HABIT?

Just 15.5 percent of us don't. The most popular seems to be tapping or jiggling our knees or legs: almost half of us—46.1 percent—are guilty. Just slightly fewer—44.5 percent—of us chew on ice and four out of 10 crack our knuckles. More than one in four of us—27.1 percent—regularly chews a pen cap or pencil. Thirty-eight percent peel the labels off bottles or cans. Three of every 10 of us twist or pull on our hair and more than one in four—26.1 percent—twists the phone cord. One of every five of us grinds our teeth. Everyone has a cousin Arthur.

DO YOU BITE YOUR NAILS?

One child in every three trims his or her overlong nails with teeth. By adulthood, it's down to one in five who say they bite their fingernails. Fewer admit to chomping on the inside of their cheek, chewing on their lips, and picking at their ears.

WHAT ABOUT YOUR TOENAILS?

One in four of us, at some point in our lives, has contorted our bodies to trim our toenails with our teeth but fewer than 1 percent of grown-ups admit they do it now.

DO YOU PICK YOUR NOSE?

Oh, if nostrils could talk, what a tale they'd tell of mauling and mistreatment. Fewer than one in 10 confess to manhandling their nasal passages but, then again, fewer than 5 percent admit to even occasionally picking their noses.

DO YOU USE A PACIFIER?

Although for a few years, wearing pacifiers was a chic inner city emblem, in fact, very few adults use them—or their equivalent. Fewer than 2 percent admit they still occasionally suck their thumbs. Compare that to two-thirds of toddlers who comfort themselves with a pacifier or fingers; by age six about one in five is still sucking a thumb. By age 11, it's down to 16 percent.

DO YOU USUALLY PICK OFF YOUR SCABS?

More than four out of every 10 of us usually pick off our scabs—with men considerably more likely than women to literally take matters into their own hands. Oddly, almost six out of every 10 left-handers have a go at their scabs while less than four out of every 10 right-handers do.

ARE YOU DOUBLE-JOINTED?

Almost 21 of every 100 women in America is apt to be double-jointed compared to 14 of every 100 men. Right-handed folks are significantly more likely than left-handed people to be double-jointed.

CAN YOU WHISTLE LOUDLY TO HAIL CABS OR OTHER PEOPLE?

Maybe whistling is related to testosterone but men are almost four times as likely as women to do it—loudly. Some 22.9 percent of men say it's part of their vocabulary; only 6.5 percent of women use it or know how. But when it comes to whistling on a blade of grass, the disparity narrows some—to slightly more than two times men's favor. Midwesterners are more likely than anyone else to whistle on grass and right-handed people are more than two times as prone to do so as lefties.

CAN YOU ROLL YOUR TONGUE?

Roughly two in three of us can roll our tongues—into a coiled U-position that is, but fewer than one in 10 can reach the tips of our nose with it. Is tongue rolling wasted on the young? Under 35s say they can do it far more than older folks, and oddly, those with young children at home, most of all. Two times as many women as men can touch their tongue to their nose, and seven times as many under 35s as their older counterparts can do so. Only 4 percent of westerners can stretch that organ.

CAN YOU WIGGLE YOUR EARS?

Maybe Bugs can do it, but few of us can. Just 13.2 percent of Americans can wiggle their ears, though westerners are more than twice as likely as northeasterners to perform this feat.

CAN YOU RAISE ONE EYEBROW AT A TIME?

Charlie Chaplin was able to levitate his tufts one at a time and three out of every 10 of us can, too. Young men, southerners, and westerners consider it a badge of some kind judging by their relative aptitude.

CAN YOU JUGGLE?

Here's another one of those things like video games and computer savvy which seem to skew toward males. Almost one in four of all men can juggle whereas in women it's closer to one in 10. It's a similar split with age (the younger, the jugglier), singlehood versus married (bachelors have their hands in lots of things!), right-handeds versus southpaws, and oddly, income level: poorer folks are twice as likely as their wealthier counterparts to know how to juggle.

CAN YOU DO A SPLIT?

All those years of ballet training and calisthetics and fewer than one in five of us can do a split. Not surprisingly, women are considerably more agile here.

CAN YOU BLOW SPIT BUBBLES?

One in five of us can, though younger folks are seven times as capable in the spit bubble blowing biz.

CAN YOU BLOW SMOKE RINGS?

Westerners cannot: more than one in five of us overall can, but just 12 percent of westerners can.

CAN YOU CROSS YOUR EYES?

Almost one in four of us can cross our eyes, with young folks far more likely to get those orbs transformed.

CAN YOU FLARE YOUR NOSTRILS?

Whoa, boy. Just about a third of us can control the nose openings to dramatic effect.

CAN YOU SNAP YOUR FINGERS?

You'd think everyone could, wouldn't you? But 32 percent of us, poor souls, can't. Southerners and southpaws have the most trouble snapping: is that why country music is full of twangs?

Cleaning

ARE YOU CLEANLINESS COMPULSIVE?

We're a veritable nation of Lady MacBeths. We rarely smell our socks before we throw them into the laundry but almost half of us claim to change our towels *daily* or after every shower.

WHICH IS WORSE—THE DIRT YOU CAN SEE, OR THE KIND YOU CAN'T?

We still believe that cleanliness is next to godliness—65 percent of women and 62 percent of men want to scour the less visible stuff. But that's way down from the more than 75 percent who felt that way a decade ago.

DO YOU MAKE YOUR BED DAILY?

Amazingly, 21 percent of us don't make our bed every day—and five percent never do! Women over 45 are far likelier than those under 45 to make their beds—71 percent versus 45 percent. And despite parental admonition, only 19 percent of children do daily. But whether they pull the corners tight, or leave it in a heap, just 15 percent feel the least bit guilty. Only 9 percent of husbands pitch in.

WHAT ABOUT THE BEDSHEETS?

Astonishingly, 3 percent of Americans (twice as many men as women) say they change their bedsheets daily—and another 14 percent, every couple of days. (Compulsive—or out of touch?) Most change them once a week.

DO YOU ALPHABETIZE YOUR BOOKS?

How can anybody find things in America? Eighty-seven percent of Americans randomly collect records, tapes, CDs, and books. Just 13 percent alphabetizes or in other ways, such as grouping by subject, categorizes their resources. Older folks (could it be their collections are larger?) are more apt to take a more orderly approach.

HOW LONG DO YOU SAVE MAGAZINES?

Till the cows come home. Fewer than 10 percent of us leave them lying around for two weeks or less. Half of us guestimate they're out of the house in six months and another 20 percent of us claim to hold on to them for years and years. Roughly 15 percent of us toss them when spring or fall cleaning inspiration strikes.

DO YOU WEAR RUBBER GLOVES TO CLEAN?

It depends on the job, but roughly half of Americans gear up to tackle the grease. Midwesterners and southerners are likelier than northeasterners or westerners to do so and those who care about their nails or who are cleaning someplace other than their own home are more likely to slip on the latex.

HAVE YOU EVER TURNED CLOTHES INSIDE OUT TO AVOID DOING LAUNDRY?

Many people were horrified at the question. They'd be more horrified at the answer: fully 12 percent of us have taken this desperate measure. Another four percent volunteered that they've worn clothes past their prime—albeit rightside up—to postpone doing the laundry. Younguns are likelier than older folks to put off the hunt for detergent by whatever means.

AND SPEAKING OF LAUNDRY, WHO DOES IT?

Men do 29 percent of the 419 million loads of laundry we wash each week. Yet only 7 percent of women trust their husbands to do it correctly. Virtually all unmarried men do at least one load a week.

Clothes

HOW OFTEN DO YOU SLIP INTO SOMETHING MORE COMFORTABLE?

Almost two-thirds of us—male and female—put on clothes in the morning and call it a day. But two out of three women slip in and out of something more (or less) comfortable at least twice a day. Fewer than one in 10 of us (including nurses, waitresses, and other uniform-wearers) puts on more than two different getups for different parts of the day.

WHAT GOES ON FIRST?

More than one of every five of us—22 percent—can't recall whether we put on our underpants, bra, or pantyhose first—or consider the request too perverse to respond to. About half of those who do know put on their panties first—49 percent—though a third of us follow that by adding the bra while 16 percent put on their hose next. For almost one in five of us—19 percent—the bra is the first thing we put on. Fifteen percent of us wear our hose *under* our panties.

MEN, DO YOU DRESS LEFT TO RIGHT?

Most men do, tailors say, but few know what it means—which is in which direction the penis lies so trousers can be slightly roomier there. In our survey, fewer than 10 percent of either sex had any idea.

CAN YOU TIE A BOW TIE?

Who'd have thought that women, more than men, know how to tie a bow tie—but that more than half the world hasn't a clue? That's why clip-ons were invented. (Specifically, 42 percent of women say they can tie a bow tie by themselves, while only 33 percent of men claim to be up to the task.)

HOW DO YOU BUTTON A SHIRT?

More than three times as many people do it from the top down as from the bottom up.

DO YOU UNTIE AND RETIE YOUR SHOES EACH TIME YOU PUT THEM ON?

Astonishingly, seven out of 10 of us do. But more than a fifth—22 percent—casually slip on their shoes without untying and retying them. Or else they favor Velcro, slip-ons, or the untied look.

WHICH SHOE GOES ON FIRST?

It's pretty much a toss-up with the right shoe very slightly edging out the left as the primo footwear. Almost three out of every four left-handed people, however, slip on their left shoe first. For the average American woman, it's a size 8B.

SPEAKING OF SHOES, HAVE YOU EVER THROWN ONE AT A MAN?

Astonishingly, four out of 10 of us—39.5 percent—admitted that they had been so mad that they had hurled footwear at an offending fellow.

AND WOULD YOU DRINK CHAMPAGNE FROM IT?

Almost one in 10—9.4 percent—of us daring and romantic souls has sipped or would sip the bubbly from a wing-tip. We are assuming, of course, that the shoe has not been worn.

HOW DO YOU STOW YOUR SOCKS?

The roll-into-a-ball approach slightly edges out folding—46 to 43 percent. Relatively few—one in six of us, though higher among young people—randomly throw our socks into the drawer.

DO YOU HANG UP YOUR CLOTHES WHEN YOU TAKE THEM OFF?

Slightly more than half of us—54 percent—are anal when it comes to our apparel. No sooner does it come off our bodies than it lands on a hanger. Others, in descending order, drape it over a clothes rack or chair, leave it curled on the floor, or kick it under the bed. Out of sight, out of mind.

DO YOU USE THE SLIT IN YOUR UNDERWEAR?

Some 85 percent of men go over it. Why go through all the trouble and expense stitching a flap if no one bothers with it?

GUYS, WHAT TYPE OF UNDERWEAR DO YOU WEAR?

Amazingly, 6.4 percent of men claim they don't wear any at all. Boxers may be the new chic but two-thirds haven't heard the news. Some 67.5 percent wear mainly briefs—because they're less wind resistant and more supportive. Northeastern men are twice as likely as midwesterners—43.6 percent to 21.6 percent—to go for boxers. President Clinton may have been tightlipped about his affairs de coeur—but not about what he was wearing when said episodes might have happened. He has revealed that more often than not he wears briefs.

LADIES, YOUR UNDERWEAR DOSSIER?

First off, some 3.9 percent of women don't wear any. Just over half—51 percent—wear briefs, 40.5 percent, bikinis (with younger women more likely) and 4.6 percent, thongs. Interestingly, women with household incomes under $40,000 are eight times likelier than wealthier women to wear thongs. Fashion statement though it may be, less than 1 percent even occasionally wears her underwear on the outside.

WHAT'S YOUR BRA SIZE?

The average bra size today is 36C. A decade ago it was 34B. Today, 12 percent of the population is an A cup, compared to 8 percent five years ago. Likewise, 30 percent is a B cup and 30 percent a C cup, compared to 35 and 33 percent, respectively, five years ago. And the number of D cups is rising—from 24 percent five years ago to 28 percent today. No, it's not breast augmentation or body shaping exercisers; aging causes breasts to droop. Manufacturers say that 85 percent of us are wearing the wrong size.

WHAT DO YOU CARRY IN YOUR BRIEFCASE OR BOOKBAG?

The bookbag is one item that hasn't outgrown its name. More than four out of five—82 percent—of people pack some sort of reading matter in their backpacks. More than half—54 percent—tote a pain reliever. Almost one in three—30 percent—also carry a snack, clothing, or condoms! Almost as many carry a self defense device—24 percent—as lug around a toothbrush—26 percent. Six percent of those sacks contain a telephone and 3 percent a laptop computer.

HOW ABOUT IN YOUR PURSE?

The average wallet contains $104 and change. In addition to a wallet, almost all of us—97 percent—carry keys, while 80 percent pack a comb and 76 percent carry checks. Some 69 percent of purses contain makeup and an address book.

DID YOU WEAR SOMETHING OLD, SOMETHING NEW, SOMETHING BORROWED, AND SOMETHING BLUE AS A BRIDE?

Just about nine of every 10 brides followed the formal prescriptives—with an heirloom blue garter satisfying three out of four requirements.

DO YOU WEAR A WEDDING BAND?

Two-thirds of married folk wear the emblem of their matrimonial status with young and baby boomer men considerably more likely than their mates to do so. Three out of four first-time brides received a diamond engagement ring—average value $1,597—and then waited a year to walk down the aisle. Three out of five stones bought were round.

WHAT OTHER JEWELRY DO YOU WEAR?

Just as most women won't leave the house sans makeup, seven out of 10 don't exit without some jewelry. Just three out of 100 say they never wear any. More of us—27 percent—wear at least five pieces of jewelry (earrings count as two). Just 6.5 percent of women wear one piece.

WHERE DO YOU WEAR YOUR WATCH?

Most people wear them on their left wrist, regardless of whether they're right- or left-handed. Fewer than two in every hundred don't wear a watch. Even though most people own 3.5 watches, they tend to wear the same one daily.

WOULD YOU WEAR JEANS TO WORK?

Some 86 percent of respondents think that neat jeans are appropriate attire for casual days at work. Some 74 percent okay athletic shoes and 32 percent consider shorts acceptable. On an average Americans wear jeans or denim shorts 4.2 days a week, with women chalking up 4.7 days/occasions and men 3.9.

WHAT'S SEXIER: SUIT, SLACKS, OR JEANS?

By a wide margin (52 percent) women prefer men in denim jeans and a casual shirt than any other garb. Some 31 percent would rather see their fellow in casual slacks and a sweater and just 17 percent opt for a suit or jacket and tie.

WHAT'S THE MAIN REASON YOU NO LONGER WEAR SOMETHING?

Stop the presses: it's not because it's gone out of style. Rather, it's because it's gone out of fit. Some 39 percent of people say they've given up wearing a garment because it's no longer comfortable while another 25 percent have jettisoned something because it's worn out or stained. Just 23 percent say they've abandoned clothing because it's out of style and 30 percent because they haven't had the right occasion to wear it.

WOULD YOU RATHER WEAR ONE OUTFIT FOR LOTS OF ACTIVITIES . . . OR CHANGE?

Assuming the outfit is comfortable, by a 62 percent to 38 percent margin, Americans would rather wear one all-purpose getup than multiple outfits.

YOU'RE IN A GREAT LOOKING SWEATER AT A HOT PARTY AND STARTING TO GET WARM. WHAT DO YOU DO?

Almost two out of three (64 percent) would take it off and be cooler. The other 36 percent would leave it on and look good.

WOULD YOU RATHER BE ON TIME AND LOOK OK . . . OR 10 MINUTES LATE AND LOOK GREAT?

No question, Americans are a punctual lot. Two-thirds (65 percent) would rather be on time and look all right than tardy and look great (35 percent).

DO YOU WANT TO BE NOTICED FOR YOUR CLOTHES?

Dolly Parton excluded, just 47 percent of women dress to be noticed. Another 52 percent would prefer people not notice their clothes. Some 41 percent of men want to be noticed for their clothes while 50 percent don't.

IF GIVEN AN EXTRA $500, WHAT PART WOULD YOU SPEND ON CLOTHES?

Almost half, say Americans. Women would spend $278 and men $202 for a mean $247.

WHERE DO YOU STOW YOUR DOUGH?

Just 61 percent of men carry a wallet—less in the city than in the country, though 96 percent of women carry a purse. One in five men throws his money loose in his pockets. Is it harder to be ripped off that way? Six percent carry a money clip and 10 percent a coin or change purse. Two percent claim they don't know how they carry their money.

IS YOUR WALLET ORGANIZED?

Reeeeeeady, march! Almost three of every four of us store our dollar bills in rigid order with singles leading up to higher denominations. (No folded or crumpled bills here.) Northerners and baby boomers of both genders are considerably more likely than southerners to stow their paper money randomly.

ETHICS

DO YOU EVER DO YOUR CHILDREN'S HOMEWORK FOR THEM OR, AHEM, SIMPLY GUIDE THEM?

No wonder Johnny got an A. Thirteen percent of us admit we occasionally do it for our offspring. Everybody else feigns horror at the thought.

IF YOU'VE DENTED ANOTHER CAR BUT NOT YOUR OWN AND YOU'RE SURE NO ONE SAW, WOULD YOU FESS UP?

Just about half of us would fade into the night. Astonishingly, men are bound by a code of ethics here: more than four out of five claim they'd leave a note on the windshield. Fewer than two of every five women would, with financially secure, college-educated women the biggest cop-out artists.

DO YOU EVER FIB?

Ever? Hah. Despite those glorifying tales about George Washington's honesty, nine out of 10 of us—91 percent—confess we lie regularly. One out of five says he or she can't get through a single day without conscious, premeditated white lies. What's more, almost half—45 percent—of us don't think lying is necessarily wrong. Another 17 percent say they don't, not because it's immoral but because they fear they'll be caught. The better we know someone, the likelier we are to have told them a serious lie.

*   *   *

Men are likelier than women to fib (or to admit it) and the younger they are, the more glib-tongued. Catholics lie a bit more than Protestants and both lie more than Jews and those out of work lie more than those working. The poor lie more than the rich and liberals more than conservatives.

WHAT'S THE BIGGEST LIE?

While we might routinely invent an identity on an airplane— 79 percent of us claim on occasion we've given a false name or phone number—we reserve our serious lying for those people we know best. But the subject about which we fib more than any other: our weight. One of every three of us admits to lying about what's on the scale—with women almost three times likelier than men to do so. Almost one in four gives out false info about what we earn, 21 percent about how old we are, and 9 percent about our true hair color.

HAVE YOU EVER CHEATED ON A QUIZ OR TEST?

More than one in four of us—27 percent—admit our eyes have roamed and pencils have copied. No telling how often.

HOW ABOUT ON YOUR TAXES?

Four out of 10 of us admit we've gotten away with all we could—and then some. A third of us exaggerate our expenses or deductions, 28 percent never even filed a return and 21 percent didn't report all the income we made. Another 18 percent counted too many dependents.

ON YOUR EXPENSE ACCOUNT?

We'd rather cheat the government than our employers. Among the rareifed group who has an expense account, 82 percent claim they never cheat. "You don't #!@/!¢$ where you eat," said one man. The few who occasionally "stretch the truth a tad" (calling lunch with a friend a business expense, for example) are more likely female. Almost 5 percent of people are so vigilant (or inattentive accounting for expenses) that they claim they lose money on the deal.

HAVE YOU EVER TRIED TO PAD AN INSURANCE BILL TO COVER YOUR DEDUCTIBLE?

Four out of 10 of us would try to inflate the bill. Men are more likely than women to submit an accurate estimate, though young men and middle-aged women are probably the biggest figure fudgers.

WHAT ABOUT ASKING A DOCTOR TO FUDGE A DIAGNOSIS SO INSURANCE PICKS IT UP?

Three out of four of us (76 percent) wouldn't dream of compromising the doc—or perhaps embarassing ourselves by claiming, say, a deviated septum for a nose job. Three percent of respondents wouldn't answer, 5 percent had no insurance, and 16 percent said they negotiate in a tactful discussion. One respondent said she never had to—doctors do it automatically. Another said a woman had to—insurance often doesn't cover routine ob/gyn visits.

HAVE YOU EVER STOLEN SOMETHING IN A STORE?

Almost one in three of us—29 percent of the population—admit they've walked out of a store without paying for something intentionally.

WHAT ABOUT STEALING THE TOWEL FROM THE HOTEL OR HEALTH CLUB?

Ever wonder why you see signs on plush terry robes that you can buy them in the gift shop—or they'll be billed to your room? Well, more than half of all guests (58 percent) *admit* they'd snatch the towel if they were sure they could get away undetected. It would probably be a lot higher for ashtrays if people still smoked.

HAVE YOU EVER SNUCK FOOD INTO A THEATER . . . OR A RESTAURANT?

Half of all Americans admit they've brought their own food into a movie—rather than pay the candy concession's lofty prices, and roughly 10 percent have done an uninvited b-y-o into a restaurant.

HOW ABOUT SNUCK INTO THE THEATER ITSELF WITHOUT PAYING?

Almost one in five of us (19 percent) has entered through the exit door or some other dodge to avoid buying a ticket. Easterners (at 26 percent) are twice as likely as southerners (13 percent) to tiptoe past the admissions booth.

DO YOU BELIEVE IN DIVINE RETRIBUTION?

Almost nine out of every 10 of us believe that all of us will eventually have to account for our actions before God (though well-heeled better educated consumers are least likely to) but two-thirds don't necessarily expect to *simmer* in Hell for our shabby behavior. The Barna Research Group of Glendale, California, found that many people living as if there's no tomorrow, are counting on a clement Being. Sixty-eight percent believe that some sins are forgivable.

DO YOU BELIEVE IN THE COMMANDMENTS? AFTERLIFE? SATAN? VOODOO?

Just one of every 10 of us believes in all of the Ten Commandments; 40 percent subscribe to five or fewer commandments. Eighty-two percent of us believe in an afterlife and 55 percent in the existence of Satan. Slightly under half expect to go to heaven and just 4 percent of us anticipate heading to the fires below. Some 45 percent of us believe in ghosts, 28 percent in witchcraft, and 20 percent in voodoo. And catch this: a fifth of us claim to have participated in a ritual of satanism or witchcraft.

HAVE YOU EVER SPENT A NIGHT IN JAIL?

An amazing 13 percent of Americans have—far more men than women—and most for very brief stays and misdemeanors.

HAVE YOU EVER SMOKED POT?

By the time most of us have reached our late 20s, more than four out of five of us have tried an illicit drug. For more than 60 percent of us, it's something stronger than marijuana. The National Institute on Drug Abuse says that almost half—48 percent—of all high schoolers have smoked pot and 29 percent have done more serious experimentation.

IS IT A SIN TO "LIVE IN SIN?"

Not anymore. Nowadays, the majority of us believes it's a good idea to live together before taking the plunge. But nearly half say that then there's no reason to get married. Fifty-nine percent believe in pre-nuptials. And in the region that includes New York and Washington, astonishingly, the rate of virgin marriages is highest—36 percent versus a national average of 29 percent.

DO YOU EVER WATER DOWN THE LIQUOR TO ACCOMMODATE MORE GUESTS?

Most of us wouldn't dream of it. But if you were to chemically analyze all the drinks you receive at a bar or party you'd discover some hosts are stretching the truth—and the goods. Some 6.1 percent of us admit we do it. Young people are five times likelier than older folks to water down the booze, singles four times likelier than marrieds to put the Chivas under the tap, and poorer folks twice as likely as the monied to stretch the Tanqueray.

EVER POUR GENERIC PRODUCTS INTO BRAND NAME CONTAINERS?

If you think that's Heinz ketchup, think again. Just about one in 10 of us empties the cheaper private label stuff into the more status-plus brand container. Midwesterners think that's cheating. Twice as many westerners and northeasterners try to pass one by, while southerners bat about average.

EVER MALINGER?

Lest we start pinning ribbons on our ethical selves, take note that almost three of every five of us—58.4 percent—have called in sick to work when we were actually fit as a fiddle. Young folks are generally looser with the medical truth than older people and those with a child at home have found the sick ruse a convenient excuse. Midwesterners are the most proper but still more than half of them have fibbed their way out of a work day.

HAVE YOU EVER TRIED TO GET OUT OF JURY DUTY?

We may pull strings to stay home from work but more than two-thirds of us claim we're Ms. and Mr. Civic, answering the call whenever summoned. Only one in four of us—27.1 percent—actually tries to finagle his or her way out of jury duty. Older folks—perhaps because they've watched the justice system at work—are almost three times more inventive at getting out than younger folks, and surprisingly, midwesterners, far from being the most upright, have come up with an excuse half the time. Men are significantly more evasive than women, trying to dodge the bullet 43 percent of the time. Most people point to work as the excuse but 14 percent cry ill, 8.3 percent small children, and 2.4 percent claim they'll be away.

WHAT WOULD YOU DO IF A CASHIER MISTAKENLY GAVE YOU MORE CHANGE THAN WAS WARRANTED?

The role model of Honest Abe seems alive and well. Only one in every five of us admit we'd keep the windfall and shut up.

The rest *say* they'd point out the error and return it. Seventy-one percent of third to eighth graders say they'd turn in $10 to their teacher if they found it on the classroom floor.

IF YOU FOUND SOMETHING WORTH $10 AND CAN FIGURE OUT WHOM IT BELONGS TO, WOULD YOU RETURN IT? WHAT ABOUT $50 OR $100?

Eighteen percent of us would think long and hard about tracking down someone to return something if they didn't know the person well and easily could get away with it. That roughly translates into keeping it. The value of the item has less impact than the relationship with the person who lost or left it.

HAVE YOU EVER SWITCHED TAGS TO PAY LESS IN THE STORE?

One in 10 of us has engaged in this sort of theft. Under 35s were three times likelier to have switched tags than over 35s and those earning under $40,000 more than twice as likely as their richer counterparts.

HOW ABOUT TO GET A BETTER FIT?

Say you're a size six top with a more ample, size 10 derriere. Some 15.5 percent of shoppers admit they'd switch tags to get different-sized, better-fitting tops and bottoms—with almost one of every four women creating the customized look for herself. Southerners were most strait laced about this—even more so than midwesterners.

HAVE YOU EVER BOUGHT SOMETHING INTENDING TO WEAR AND THEN RETURN IT?

Astonishingly, almost one in 10 of us has purchased something we intend to wear once and then return—and most don't feel much guilt about it. Almost three times as many younger people as older admit they "buy" something for a one-time fling.

HOW DO YOU FEEL ABOUT SPANKING?

Despite years of admonition from Dr. Spock and other parenting experts, more than half of us feel that a good slap on the buttocks (never the face) is a good tool in the parental arsenal. Half of us think a child younger than two shouldn't be spanked.

HAVE YOU RETURNED YOUR CENSUS FORM BY ITS DUE DATE?

Claim all you want but the government's got your number. In the last count fewer than two-thirds (63 percent) of us responded in time. Some 37 million households did not comply. Yet more than 90 percent insist they mailed the form in.

DO YOU GIVE TO CHARITY?

Just over a third—35 percent—of us open our hearts—and wallets—at least once a month. Northeasterners are more generous than anyone else.

HOW FAR WOULD YOU GO FOR $10 MILLION?

Most of us would do just about anything. A quarter of us would abandon all our friends and our church, become a woman of the street for a week, or even undergo a race or sex change. And 7 percent—one of every 14 of us—would even murder for money. Astonishingly, we'd do all of this for as little as $3 million—but not $2 million. Go figure.

FOOD FETISHES

WHICH DO YOU EAT FIRST, THE FROSTING OR THE CAKE?

Astonishingly, fewer than 3 percent of us eat them together. Most people—69 percent—took Marie Antoinette's infamous words literally: they eat cake first. Just shy of 30 percent— with younger people more inclined—pluck off the frosting first. Southerners are more into delayed gratification than anyone else: 83 percent eat the cake first.

HOW DO YOU EAT AN OREO?

Half of all Americans eat their Oreos whole, undoctored. (Collectively we scarf down 16 billion of them a year.) Of the half who pull them apart, 35 percent prefer to twist them and 30 percent to dunk them. Women are predominately twisters, and men dunkers. Sixteen percent describe themselves as nibblers. Some 19 percent of munchers claim to doctor the cookie with ice cream, peanut butter, bananas, or even chili, steak sauce, or tuna salad, or to do some multi-layer construction or smash them.

DO YOU WIND YOUR SPAGHETTI OR CUT IT?

It's pretty much a wash with slightly more than half the population twirling their stringy pasta. But here's a generational issue if there ever was one. The bulk of older eaters cut it.

WHICH COMES FIRST, THE YOLK OR THE ALBUMEN?

When eating a soft-boiled egg, almost half of us—48 percent—save the yolk for last. Some 28 percent scarf down the yellow part first and just 10 percent mash the white and yellow stuff together. Another 14 percent wouldn't touch a soft-boiled egg with any length pole.

HOW DO YOU SWALLOW AN ASPIRIN OR OTHER PILL?

Not like a man, that's for sure. Admittedly only 1 percent dissolve it in liquid or mash it up, but only three of every 100 of us say they swallow it dry. Ninety-three percent of us pop it with water, juice, or other beverage.

WHEN NO ONE'S AROUND, DO YOU TAKE IT STRAIGHT FROM THE CARTON?

Truth be told, when no one's looking, a good many of us—particularly men—figure, why bother with a dish? More than half of us (47 percent) drink straight from the carton and dip into ice cream right out of the container. Men are far likelier to guzzle milk (39.5 percent) or juice (54.1 percent) straight from the container than the more proper distaff side. Only 21.6 percent of women drink milk straight from the carton and 36.6 percent do juice that way.

DO YOU LET YOUR PEAS MIX WITH YOUR CARROTS?

So many of us are secret fetishists. Three out of 10 of us—29.4 percent—segregate our foods, keeping the rice apart from the meat. It seems those under 35 would welcome dinnerware with ridged compartments: they're 16 percent more totalitarian about the boundaries on their china than older folks.

DO YOU EAT IN A PARTICULAR ORDER?

Some 31 percent of us eat our meals in a distinct order—either all of one offering first or in a fixed pattern. Southerners are the most relaxed about this whereas children and southpaws are the most rigid.

DO YOU LEAVE FOOD OVER?

Virtually no one leaves food on their plates at home—but when eating out or at someone's home, 6 percent of us remember our early etiquette manuals and leave a morsel or two on our plate for politeness's sake. Midwesterners are more than three times likelier than northeasterners to do so.

IF YOU TASTED SOMETHING YOU HATED, WHAT WOULD YOU DO?

One in five of us would swallow it. The majority would tactfully ease it into a napkin but almost one in six of us—even more among westerners—would spit it right out.

WHO SEASONS FIRST? (AND WHO'S SORRY NOW?)

One in five of us regularly salts sans sampling—more likely men than women. Ruralites are twice as likely as city dwellers to season before they taste. Between the ages of 30 and 80, people lose 64 percent of their taste buds.

DRESSING . . . ON THE SIDE?

Women are far likelier than men to order salad dressing on the side—though fewer than a third exercise this portion control.

WHAT'S YOUR EGG QUOTIENT?

Eggs used to be as American as apple pie and hamburgers. But while beef has bounced back, cholesterol laden eggs are in the doghouse. Most of us have a meal with eggs seven times a month—compared to 12 times a month a decade ago. Top styles are scrambled and sunny-side—preferred by 12 percent and 11 percent of the population, respectively. Some 15 percent of people douse their eggs with ketchup.

HAVE YOU EVER EATEN SPAM?

The thought of it sends chills up the spine of fewer than 15 percent of us. Hormel, which makes the mystery luncheon meat, says 60 million of us will eat it this year.

HOW DO YOU TAKE YOUR COFFEE?

A third of Americans don't drink coffee at all. Those who do quaff an average 1.87 cups a day. Men drink more coffee (2.11 cups) in a day than women (1.6 cups), and 40- to 49-year-olds more than anyone else (2.62 cups a day). Half of all coffee drinkers take it black.

AND O.J.?

Maybe Simpson will have a negative ripple effect on what has been virtually our national juice but until now seven out of 10 people say they drink orange juice almost daily. On average we down 32 quarts of the stuff a year—compared to say, 50 quarts of milk, 4 pounds of butter, and 46 quarts of popcorn.

DO YOU EAT ICE CREAM OR FROZEN YOGURT?

Given a choice between cake and ice cream, just 29 percent of us would rather eat cake. But that doesn't mean we'll settle for ice milk or yogurt: despite all the talk of fat free, three times as many Americans scarf down ice cream several times a week (24 percent) as go whole hog on yogurt (7 percent). The normal red-blooded American scarfs down 23 quarts of ice cream a year.

DO YOU WAIT FOR THE ICE CREAM TO THAW—OR ATTACK?

On the whole, we're twice as likely to eat ice cream while frozen than wait for it to thaw. But 18 percent of the population admits they're so impatient they often hurry the process along by zapping it in the microwave.

WHAT'S YOUR FAVORITE FLAVOR?

Hands down, despite all the new concoctions, it's still vanilla. One of every four ice cream servings is vanilla while chocolate accounts for less than one in 10 (9 percent). The average household freezer contains two or three packs of different brands or flavors. By a wide margin women more than men prefer exotic flavors.

WHAT ABOUT CANDY?

We eat more Snickers than any other candy, followed by M&M's and Hershey Almond. Averaged out, we down 16.3 pounds of chocolate a year. Easterners prefer dark chocolate but the rest of the country opts for milk chocolate.

WHAT COLOR M&M'S DO YOU PREFER?

Surprisingly, brown. Mars, the maker of M&M's, which sprinkles its color assortment based on regular consumer preference tests, loads the bag of its plain variety with 30 percent brown and 20 percent each of yellows and reds. Each bag contains roughly 10 percent each of green, orange, and tan coated chocolates.

Recently Mars ran a color preference poll and found Americans prefer blue to pink or purple. In 1995, blue will replace tan.

DO YOU SAMPLE UNINVITED?

More than four out of 10 of us would dip into someone else's plate—uninvited—with women more than men thinking it's their God-given right to sample. Oddly, left-handed individuals are almost 20 percent more likely to angle a fork toward someone else's plate to sample.

WILL YOU INTERCEPT THAT FORK COMING TO SAMPLE SOMETHING ON YOUR PLATE?

Almost three of every five of us are irked (albeit, nonviolently) when someone eats off our plate. Northeasterners take umbrage more than other folks and older people more than younger.

DO YOU SKIP MEALS? WHICH ONE?

For all the heat breakfast takes, it's lunch that more of us skip. On any given day more than one in five of us—22 percent—forgo lunch while less than one in 10—9 percent—passes up breakfast. Two-thirds of us regularly eat cereal—67 percent—and more than a third—36 percent—take toast. Nine percent of the population regularly eats pancakes, sausages, and waffles. A "normal" person spends just over an hour a day chowing down.

HOW MANY CEREALS IN YOUR CUPBOARD?

Just about half of Americans figure they have only one or two. Yet the cereal companies claim that the average cupboard contains four different brands. Women eat hot wheat cereal almost one and a half times more often than men.

DESSERT ANYONE?

When they wheel around the dessert tray, men are far likelier than women—particularly coastal ones—to order a sweet in a restaurant. But don't try to foist any wimpy raspberries or strawberries on them.

WHAT'S YOUR FAVORITE FRUIT?

We don't name it but do we ever buy it. Bananas are, well, top banana. They have replaced grapefruits as the best-selling fruit in the store. Women are 17 percent more likely than men to eat fruit—but some varieties are more acceptable to men. While 50 percent more women than men would eat cantaloupe, considerably more males than females eat fruit cocktail and raisins. Fewer than one in five of us follow the nation's recommended nutrition advice—of eating five servings of fruit and veggies a day—including one in five doctors. One in five of us eats no fruit at all and 15 percent rarely touch a vegetable other than potatoes.

WHAT'S YOUR FAVORITE BEVERAGE?

If that means what do you drink most with dinner, the answer, surprisingly, is milk, not soft drinks. Some 24 percent of suppers include a glass of the white stuff compared to 14 percent for soda.

WHAT'S YOUR FAVORITE RESTAURANT FOOD?

Hands down, more people order french fries at a restaurant than any other food. Twenty-two percent of all restaurant meals include them. Hamburgers are the second most popular with 17 percent of us ordering them. Most of us take our fries plain but almost two out of five of us flavor them. Ketchup is the most popular flavoring—but vinegar and, gulp, mayonnaise, are also big. Incidentally, the average restaurant check: $3.98 a person, says the National Restaurant Association. Not exactly the Ritz.

WHAT DO YOU PUT ON YOUR BURGER?

Less than a third of us—30 percent—grace it with ketchup. In the Northeast, however, burgers and ketchup go together like love and marriage. In the Southwest, mayonnaise and mustard are equally important.

ASSUME MONEY'S NO OBJECT. WHAT WOULD YOU ORDER IN A RESTAURANT?

Americans must consider the bad rap steak has taken to be a bum steer. Steak remains the first choice for most of us eating out. It's bigger with men than with women, strongest of all in the Midwest and South, and a home run with teens. It's least popular in the East where, when folks do order it, they like it rare. So do rich folks. In the rest of the country, medium is the degree of doneness requested most often. Men are 20 percent more likely than women to use steak sauce.

YOUR TURN, KIDS.

It's pbjs all the way. Some 28 percent of children say peanut butter and jelly sandwiches are their favorite lunch followed by bologna, picked by 14 percent, ham and cheese and hamburgers, selected by 11 percent each, and grilled cheese, turkey, and tuna, tapped by 5 percent each.

PIZZA PREFERENCES?

Most people prefer it piping hot, though 15 out of every 100 of us prefer pizza refrigerator temperature. Those earning less than $40,000 annually are more than twice as likely as richer folks to prefer it chillingly chilled. The thought of cold pizza makes southerners shudder. About four times as many northeasterners eat it cold as southerners and more than twice as many right-handers as left prefer it that way.

WHAT UTENSILS DO YOU USE TO EAT PIZZA?

For four out of five of us—81 percent—hands will do just fine, but roughly one in five attacks pizza with a knife and fork. They are primarily midwesterners.

HOW DO YOU DEAL WITH THE TOPPINGS?

More than one of every five of us pick the toppings off the pizza before downing it. Women are twice as likely as men to do so and younger folks and marrieds are much likelier than olders and singles to do so.

AND IF THERE'S ONE SLICE OF A PIE LEFT?

Almost one in five of us—19 percent—believe if there's one slice of pizza left and more than one prospective mouth into which it might go, it's every man for himself. While the vast majority, including young folks, claim they ask and offer it, one out of four adults with children at home just grabs. As a rule, men believe the slice should go to the one who's quickest on the draw.

DO YOU EAT CORN ON THE COB METHODICALLY?

More than half of us—58.4 percent—eat the yellow stuff row by row compared to 36 percent who eat corn randomly. Interestingly, westerners are quite rigid about their maize, approaching it linerally, while southerners and men are much more relaxed.

DO YOU USUALLY SWALLOW THE SEEDS WHEN EATING WATERMELON?

While 14 of every 100 of us swallow the seeds, only 7 percent of those from Dixie and 6.4 percent of those from the Northeast do. Those macho westerners are almost four times likelier to down the seeds as the population on the whole.

HOW DO YOU USUALLY OPEN NUTS?

Whatever did they invent the nutcracker for? Fewer than half—43.2 percent—of Americans ever use it. And why should they when they've got their fingers and their teeth? Some 28.4 percent pry nuts apart and one in four bites them open with their teeth—with southerners more than twice as likely as midwesterners to do so.

WHAT HANGS ON YOUR REFRIGERATOR DOOR?

The fridge is more than a storage bin for food. It's the family museum. In almost four of every 10 homes in America—36.5 percent—photographs hang there and in one of four so do children's artwork. Some 37.1 percent of us hang "to do" lists on our fridges and 10.3 percent assemble the bills there too.

DO YOU LIKE TO COOK?

Fifty-six percent of men and 78 percent of women claim they love to cook. Oddly, the number of women saying so has steadily dropped since 1975 while the number of men making the claim has steadily increased. Eighty-four percent of women and 32 percent of men have baked "from scratch" with just a third of women and 6 percent of men doing it a dozen times or more a year.

GROOMING

HOW DO YOU BRUSH YOUR PEARLY WHITES?

Contrary to popular opinion, the whole world does *not* brush their teeth up and down; slightly less than half do, though most of those are older folks. Roughly one in four of us aims to whiten and brighten in a fastidious circular motion; far less (13 percent) do it from side to side. Fewer do it back and forth, fewer still on an angle, or with an electric brush; and yes, some even "soak."

HOW OFTEN DO YOU USE MOUTHWASH?

Apparently, a third of us have never heard the word *halitosis.* At least we don't do anything about it. But for 5 percent, it's an obsession. These swishers and swillers use the stuff three or four times a day. The bulk of us—45 percent, led primarily by midwesterners—use it every day or twice a day.

HOW DO YOU SQUEEZE THE TUBE?

Who'd have thought that women were the ones infuriatingly squeezing the toothpaste tube from the middle? Or worse, from the top! Still, more than half of both sexes say they aim for the bottom.

DO YOU REPLACE THE CAP ON THE TOOTHPASTE TUBE?

Most people, even including young folks, cap the Crest. The slobs among us have suddenly gone mute.

DO YOU ALWAYS RINSE OUT THE TOOTHPASTE REMAINS FROM THE SINK?

More than one in five of us—22 percent—confess we sometimes leave the glop in the basin, a little gift for the next person!

DO YOU FLOSS?

Americans know they should floss and feel so guilty about their failure to do so that they lie. By one estimate 12 percent of people actually do floss. Four of every 10 Americans we surveyed claimed to do it daily. One in five (17 percent) admits they never floss. Women and older folks are more likely to floss; those earning under $15,000 a year, least likely. Not surprisingly, most of us floss in the bathroom. But—news flash—commercial TV breaks are not just good for going to the bathroom: 5 percent of us practice our dental hygiene then.

HAVE YOU EVER FLOSSED WITH YOUR HAIR?

Seven out of 100 admit we have, with westerners more than four times as likely as midwesterners. Almost one in four has also picked his or her teeth with a match.

AN APPLE A DAY KEEPS THE DOCTOR AWAY, BUT HOW ABOUT A BATH OR SHOWER?

Three out of four of us—76 percent—regularly take showers. While most women still prefer showers, more women take baths than men (28 versus 22 percent.) These major ablutions, of course, are supplemented by 6.8 trips a day to the bathroom sink for face/hand washing—or 45 trips a week, according to Lever Bros.

HOW OFTEN?

At least two-thirds of us bathe or shower once a day—but 15 percent of us could really use a good scrub. Winter or summer, these water- and soap-averse folks can't be coaxed in more than once every other day. And then there are the Lady MacBeths who take this cleanliness-is-next-to-godliness thing to the nth degree. Five percent of us ablute two or three times a day; presumably, (one hopes) after workouts.

HOW LONG DOES YOUR SHOWER LAST?

Most of us say it takes approximately 10 minutes: teen girls figure they spend at least 15 minutes there. But research from Lever Bros. determined the actual shower takes 4 minutes—and that the typical water temperature is 101 degrees Fahrenheit.

WHERE DO YOU PICK YOUR NOSE—AND HOW DO YOU DISPOSE OF BOOGIES?

Women who will allow videocams to record them delivering babies won't fess up on this—the last taboo. Most people insist they always use a Kleenex *and* retreat to the loo, shower, or some other private place. Many stonewall, saying they never pick their nose—don't even know they have one. (What a contrary twisted tale of torture our nasal passages could tell.) Fewer than 10 percent admit they let their fingers do the digging and some confess they drop the remains on the floor or flick them across the room—though only in extremely dry atmospheres.

DO YOU DRY YOUR HAIR WITH THE BLOWER OR NATURAL AIR?

Roughly half of us brave the electromagnetic currents for vanity's sake; the rest let nature take its course. (Almost one in four of us uses a curling iron, 12 percent electric curlers, and 16 percent hair rollers. Fifteen percent of us also use a styling comb.)

DO YOU BRUSH OR COMB . . . OR SOMETHING IN BETWEEN?

Our implement of choice to neaten hair is the brush, though 9 percent of us primarily use a pick and another 5 percent, our hands. Some 28 percent are comb loyal; those are largely men.

HOW WOULD YOU WASH THAT MAN/WOMAN RIGHT OUT OF YOUR HAIR?

The bulk of us would do it in the shower. A measly 4 percent of us wash our hair reclining comfortably in the bath. Another 10 percent do it bent over the sink. Men claim to shampoo their hair almost uniformly in the shower; women say they wash their hair in three out of every four showers.

Most of us get down to business at the start of our ablutions, but twice as many men as women do it at the end. Some 61 percent of women wash their heads as soon as they turn on the tap versus 49 percent of men, and only 16 percent of women wait until the end, while 35 percent of men do.

ARE YOU LOSING IT?

We all are, more or less, losing it. Over a lifetime, the size of the hairs on most of our heads shrink 20 percent, resulting in a flat, limp look. But more than a third of women—and just about two-thirds of men—are seriously losing their hair. The *normal* head—if you're blond that means around 120,000 strands, brunette, 100,000, and carrotheads, 80,000—sheds 50 to 100 hairs a day. Those on balding domes don't grow back. Almost half of all men start balding by their 30s; by age 80, most pates are bare.

. . . AND WHAT ARE YOU DOING ABOUT IT?

Two out of five men with high hair loss—41 percent—wear hats and caps—almost twice the 23 percent of those with low hair loss who do. More than a third—36 percent—grow a beard or mustache to cover this follicular deficit, compared to 18 percent of men with little hair loss.

HOW'S THIS DEAL: A FULL HEAD OF HAIR FOR FIVE YEARS OF YOUR LIFE?

While three out of four say you can keep your magic potion, amazingly, a quarter of men want a full healthy head of head for life so much they'd seriously consider the deal—or take it. Was Daniel Webster bald?

DOES SHE OR DOESN'T SHE?

Nearly a third of women in America color their hair. That figure virtually doubles for working women in their 30s, 40s, and 50s. The median age for starting to dye is 36, to create special effects, 27. Some 69 percent of us have naturally brown hair.

ARE YOU FLAKY?

Either that or there's snow on your black jacket. More than half of us at some point in our lives have dandruff, especially when we're stressed out. Men as well as those in puberty with active oil glands are far likelier than the very young or old to shed. Those who live in sunny warm spots are least likely to flake.

IF THAT FOUNTAIN OF YOUTH EXISTED, WOULD YOU DRINK?

Ponce de Leon, look out. Two-thirds of us—64 percent— would prefer to *look* young more than to think it, and would knock each other down rushing to get there with gallon jugs.

HAVE YOU HAD—OR PLAN TO HAVE—COSMETIC SURGERY?

Nine percent of women and 8 percent of men have either already gone under the knife or are seriously contemplating some sort of optional surgical nip and tuck.

EVER LEAVE THE HOUSE WITH YOUR BIRTHDAY FACE?

More than half of us would rather eat glass. Fifty-three percent wear makeup all the time—and 45 percent spend at least

15 minutes a day applying it. But half of us say that when the weekend rolls around, they often go unadorned.

IF YOU HAD TO FORFEIT ONE ITEM OF MAKEUP, WHAT WOULD IT BE?

Apparently not mascara or blush, our first line of defense. More than four out of five of us—82 percent—rely on those more than anything else, followed by lipstick, the number one pick of 75 percent, and eyeshadow, the top selection of 71 percent. Most women use five cosmetic products every morning.

DO YOU OPEN YOUR MOUTH WHEN YOU APPLY MASCARA?

Many more women gape—28 percent—while working away with those wands than apply mascara tight-lipped (16 percent). But four of every 10 of us don't know and can't visualize what we do with the rest of our face when lengthening our lashes. L'Oreal's Beauty Response Test Center in New York says the average woman runs the mascara wand over her lashes more than 300 times each morning!

HOW ABOUT PURSE YOUR LIPS WHEN YOU APPLY LIPSTICK?

Although in movies the woman usually purses her lips when she puts on lipstick, in reality, few—just 6 percent—do. Half the lipstick appliers—57 percent—keep their mouth slightly ajar and some "stretch their lips out" (17 percent). But most— 19 percent—haven't a clue how the color gets on their lips.

DO YOU PAINT YOUR NAILS?

More than half of us—58 percent—claim we do so regularly. Women with jobs outside the home are 20 percent more likely to polish. Even men are into the act. Six percent of straight rural men use nail polish.

Just 2 percent of American women get a professional manicure each week, only 15 percent get one even occasionally, and

81 percent have never had one. According to *American Salon,* 90,000 manicurists nationally will do around 81 million pairs of hands this year at an average of $8.20 a visit. They will also administer some 20 million pedicures at an average cost of roughly $17. The pampered probably wait until after the lacquer is applied to pay.

DO YOU K.O. B.O.?

Nine out of 10 of us never want to let them see us sweat. More than 90 percent of women roll, spray, or slick on an antiperspirant to get rid of body odor. But only 62 percent of men opt for a deodorant.

DO YOU DOUCHE?

Almost four in 10 women douche—but 6 percent don't know if they do and 7 percent refuse to tell. Half of those who do use a home-concocted solution.

DO YOU SQUEEZE YOUR ZITS?

Sixty-two percent of us squeeze. Men are slightly more likely than women—65 to 60 percent—to bring matters to a head. Eighty percent of midwesterners squeeze, while only 60 percent of northeasterners do.

HOW ABOUT FACIALS?

Almost a third of women—32 percent—get facials. Twelve percent of men also do.

HOW DO YOU FEEL ABOUT RIP VAN WINKLE?

The average Joe spends 3,350 hours of his life shaving 16,000 odd strands—that grow 5.5 inches a year and cover 48 square inches. Ninety percent of American men shave regularly—on average 24 times a month. Fifty-four percent of women and 49 percent of men feel all men should be clean shaven every day.

DO YOU LATHER UP OR PLUG IN?

Gillette says just 22 percent of male shavers use electric razors. Those who lather up invariably hang around the sink. While most plug-in shavers stay in the bathroom, they often roam into the bedroom or even the kitchen with the thunderous whine signaling their approach.

WHAT WOULD YOU CHANGE ABOUT YOURSELF PHYSICALLY?

If we could change one thing about our faces or bodies most of us would drop some pounds. More than half of us want to change our tonnage. Another 32 percent want to doctor their bodies, their age, or their intelligence, and a fifth of us would love to change our height or our hair. More than half of us—54.3 percent—would rather get run over by a truck than gain 150 pounds.

HOW OFTEN DO YOU WEIGH YOURSELF?

Five percent of Americans are truly weight obsessed: they're on the scale *more than once a day.* Another 8.1 percent weigh themselves daily and 10 percent do so at least twice a week. The most frequent frequency: 36.5 percent of us weigh ourself twice a month. Slightly more do it once a year versus once a week and almost 10 percent of us—male and female—claim we *never* step on a scale. Pounds seem to be on the mind more of women than men: compulsive scale watchers are three times likelier to be female.

WHEN DO YOU WEIGH YOURSELF?

Morning has it hands down. Perhaps because we think we weigh less when we just get up and want to delude ourselves about our *avoir dupois,* roughly three times as many people (and four times as many women) weigh themselves in the morning than at night.

WHAT DO YOU WEAR WHEN YOU WEIGH YOURSELF?

A third of Americans claim it's a pretty casual encounter—that they step on the scale with whatever they happen to have on at the time. But one in five of us strips naked—not even a watch or earrings—and another 7 percent get nude but leave on the jewelry. A fifth of us keep on our clothes but kick off our shoes, and another fifth get down to our undies.

DO YOU CONSIDER VANITY A DIRTY WORD?

Collagen Corp. claims that 75 percent of Americans don't. In fact, they consider it the least negative of the Seven Deadly Sins, and perhaps even a virtue. Eleven times as many people would rather be called vain than selfish (33 percent versus 3 percent) and almost 17 times as many would opt for vain over unkind (3 percent versus 50 percent). Vain is even preferable to dull by a margin of more than four to one (13 percent versus 3 percent).

WOULD YOU RATHER BE 50 POUNDS OVERWEIGHT OR INFLICTED WITH GENITAL HERPES?

Some 91 percent would rather be 50 pounds heavier than they should, than have genital herpes.

WOULD YOU RATHER HAVE A LARGE VISIBLE RUN IN YOUR PANTYHOSE OR A PAINFUL CORN ON YOUR TOE?

Only 20 percent of women would rather suffer and look good than vice versa. As for men, 55 percent would choose a split in their pants over that painful corn (19 percent).

HAVE YOU EVER SPENT MORE THAN $50 ON A HAIRCUT?

Some 18 percent of us admit to having shelled out more than $50 on a haircut (though just 7.5 percent of men).

DO YOU REGULARLY PLUCK YOUR BROWS?

Some 43 percent of women and 7.5 percent of men regularly pluck their eyebrows.

WHAT HAVE YOU DONE TO LOSE WEIGHT?

Some 24 percent have fasted for a day or more to shed pounds (32.5 percent of women and 10 percent of men) and 32 percent have popped diet pills (45 percent of women and 7.5 percent of men).

HAVE YOU LIED ABOUT YOUR WEIGHT?

While 13 percent have lied to someone about their looks prior to a face-to-face meeting, 14 percent about their age, 33 percent have fibbed about their weight. Some 17.5 percent of men admit to having done all three while 10 percent of women have fibbed about their looks or age—and 42 percent about their *avoir dupois.*

WOULD YOU RATHER GO WITHOUT YOUR DUSTBUSTER OR BLOW-DRYER?

It seems many of us would rather have our living spaces look good than ourselves. More would choose to do without their blow-dryer (54 percent) than give up their Dustbuster (41 percent), though women are 55 percent to 45 percent more willing to dispense with the portable vac.

HOW ABOUT THE BATHROOM SCALE OR MICROWAVE?

Given a choice between the bathroom scale and the microwave, convenience wins over obsession. Some 35 percent would choose to go without their microwave and 63 percent without a bathroom scale.

HEALTH TIDBITS

HOW DO YOU APPLY A BAND-AID?

The overwhelming majority of us—three out of four with women and northeasterners more likely than men and mid-westerners—remove the paper before applying the pad. But close to a third of men use part of the adhesive strip to cover the wound while applying it. Two percent claim to never use Band-Aids at all; they just let it bleed.

HAVE YOU HAD AN OUT-OF-BODY EXPERIENCE?

Roughly one in 10 of us claims to have seen a ghost, and one in five has sensed a strange presence in the room with them. More than half of us have experienced deja vu (57 percent) and believe in the devil (55 percent) and almost as many (49 percent) believe in ESP. Seven percent insist they've seen UFOs.

HOW OFTEN ARE YOU SICK?

The "normal" child catches 6 to 10 colds a year; the "normal" adult, slightly more than 1. Boys get more colds than girls, women more than men, and older folks the fewest, from built-up immunity. People get fewer colds when the economy isn't healthy. (To save money they stay home and sulk rather than mingle socially and mix germs.) More colds seem to begin on a

Monday: they're actually "caught" (by touching the hand of someone who has one) two or three days earlier after a hard work week has lowered our resistance to infection.

The average worker calls in less than four sick days a year—with southerners, westerners, poor folk, and those nearing retirement or job changes taking off the most. Oddly, despite their neither-snow-nor-rain motto, postal workers take the greatest number of sick days, says the Bureau of Labor Statistics.

BOTHERED BY BACKACHES?

Some 56 percent have considered everything from lying on tennis balls to acupuncture for their aching backs.

MUSCLE, JOINT, OR STOMACH PAINS?

In the course of a year just about half of us suffer stomach, muscle, or joint ache.

ALLERGIES?

Ha choo! That's the sound of spring to an allergy sufferer—or some 22 million of us with hay fever. The National Institute of Allergy and Infectious Diseases says 41 million of us have allergies and/or asthma. If one of our parents had it, we've a one in four chance of developing it. If both parents suffer, so will two out of three of their children.

EVER HAD HEMORRHOIDS?

Four out of five of us—especially those who have given birth—have learned the meaning of humiliating irritation. Even Napoleon supposedly suffered a crushing defeat at Waterloo because of these "painful swollen tissues."

BEEN IMPOTENT?

Experts say 10 million men can't stay erect until ejaculation but every man, if he's honest, will confess to an impotence episode at least once in his life. (Few men are honest.)

DO YOU DO A BREAST SELF-EXAM AT LEAST ONCE A MONTH?

They may not be entirely sure exactly what they're looking for but one in every two women tries to do what the doctor ordered.

WHEN DID YOU START MENSTRUATING?

The average girl gets her first period at age 12. Assuming a woman has a 28-day cycle, which is average, and no pregnancies, which isn't, she can expect to have approximately 510 periods in her lifetime. The average period lasts five days. Approximately 70 percent of menstruating women use tampons.

DO YOU HAVE HOT FLASHES?

Assuming, of course, that you're menopausal. The average woman gets her last period at 51 and roughly 80 percent experience hot flashes. A typical flash last 2.7 minutes.

DO YOUR FEET HURT?

By Jove, they do for four out of five of us. The American Orthopedic Foot and Ankle Society says that four out of five women complain of some problem with their feet—bunions, hammertoes, calluses, you name it. The culprit is usually tight, tapered shoes. (Each foot has 26 bones, 33 joints, and 19 muscles—and walks an average 115,000 miles a lifetime.)

ARE YOU FLAT-FOOTED?

Maybe not completely but six out of 10 of us have pancake feet. The 40 percent with high arches tend to be Nordics. People from Africa and the Mediterranean tend to have low arches.

EVER HAD ATHLETE'S FOOT?

Almost half of all the men in America (46 percent) have been bedeviled by this fungus. But only 14 percent of women have had red, itchy, burning feet and cracked skin between their toes. But don't treat the condition as some sort of badge of athleticism: everyone's at risk and more than one in four (27 percent) don't know how they got it.

HOW MANY CAVITIES DO YOU HAVE IN A YEAR?

Look kids, no cavities! The annual per capita filling rate has dropped to 0.6—half what it was three decades ago—despite the fact that we visit the dentist more than then. In fact, we're four times as likely to sit near the drill now than we were in 1959. Half of school kids today have never had a cavity compared to 28 percent two decades ago.

ARE YOU FOOD ALLERGIC?

The more appropriate question might be, are you a hypochondriac? Some 17 percent of us believe we're allergic to some food (dairy products being the most widely reported—by 42 percent—followed by fruits—22 percent—seafood and vegetables—19.7 and 19.2 percent—and chocolate—8.3 percent). Yet scientific studies show only 2 percent is really allergic. Women are more allergy-minded, with west coasters seemingly more prone than southeasterners.

EVER BROKEN A BONE?

Just under half of us—44 percent—have ever broken a bone—more than twice as many who have gotten sick from food poisoning. The most frequent fractured bone is the metatarsal in the foot.

DO YOU KNOW YOUR CHOLESTEROL COUNT?

Everyone knows they should know their cholesterol blood level but only a third of us do—this despite the fact that 60 percent of us have had it checked during the past year. The National Center for Health Statistics estimates that half of all Americans have elevated levels, making them at risk for coronary heart disease.

EVER ATTENDED A SELF-HELP GROUP?

Just 14 percent of us admit we've gone to such a support group (though in the land of Woody Allen neurosis it *must* be higher). Drug and alcohol related programs are the most frequented followed by church and Bible study groups, weight loss programs, and mental health and grief support groups.

DO YOU GO TO A SHRINK?

Fifteen out of every 100 of us are in analysis or regularly go to a psychiatrist. Twenty percent of middle income people—those earning $30,000 to $50,000—go.

DONE A HOME DIAGNOSTIC TEST?

More than four out of five—82 percent of women—have learned whether they'd soon be moms without going to the doctor's office.

WHAT MAKES YOUR TUMMY QUEASY?

Anything with eggs, needles, and blood leads the list of what makes us nauseated. Other things that set off the quake: bus exhaust, day old grits, cigarette butts in a coffee cup, cat hairballs, hearing about plastic surgery, and the smell of roasting chestnuts.

WHAT MAKES YOU SWEAT?

For almost half the men in America (43.9 percent) it's getting hitched, compared to 37.6 percent of women. Divorce also causes serious alarm: 34.6 percent of men (and 31.2 percent of women) say the thought of it triggers a gush of perspiration. First dates are pretty nerve-racking to 33.1 percent of us and going to the dentist sends 35.9 percent into paroxysms. But what *really* causes a deodorant attack is making a speech: 44.7 percent of men and 53 percent of women consider that the most daunting of all prospects. To deal with the agony, more people bathe or shower than have sex, exercise, eat, shop, and drink.

ARE YOU A WALK-FAST, EAT-ON-THE-RUN, DO-TWO-THINGS-AT-A-TIME KIND OF GUY?

Chances are, if you live in the Northeast, you're likelier to be a Type A than if you come from elsewhere in America. But worldwide, the Japanese have us beat hands down—with the quickest postal clerks, most accurate bank clocks, and fastest walkers anywhere.

WOULD YOU RATHER END UP IN SHADY ACRES OR DIE QUICKLY?

More than four times as many of us, 78 percent versus 16 percent, would rather be hit by a bus or die from a fast-acting disease than end up in a "retirement home." This despite the fact that two-thirds of us long to make it to 100.

DO YOU CARRY SOME SELF-DEFENSE DEVICE?

Almost half of all women—46 percent—at least sometimes carry mace, hot pepper spray, a stilleto-sharp nail file, or a hat pin to defend themselves. A goodly proportion confess they aren't sure they'd have the presence of mind to use it. Many others say they got a dog to provide protection. Four percent of us carry a whistle or other noisemaking device to summon help.

WHAT ARE OUR ODDS?

That we'll make it out of this world alive: zero. That we'll make it through the year: pretty good. One in 115 of us will die—two-thirds will be the victims of heart disease or a violent crime; one in three of us will be injured this year, and one in 12 will have an auto accident. One in 77 of us over 35 will have a heart attack. One in 350,000 of us will be electrocuted and one in 2 million will die from falling out of bed.

IN THE JOHN

HOW DO YOU DEAL WITH TOILET PAPER?

In the john we're definitive. We care. More of us (especially men) fold the "toilet tissue" rather than bunch it up or wrap it around our hand. More than half regularly insert the roll so the paper will be pulled from over the top. A fourth insists on the underneath pull. Only 8 percent don't know or care how the paper unfolds.

MEN, DO YOU LEAVE THE TOILET SEAT DOWN AFTER YOU'VE PEED?

Why is it that if 46.5 percent of men say they always put the seat down after they've used the john, women *always* find it up? Just 14.6 percent of men say they invariably leave the seat in the position where they've last used it. Westerners and northeastern men seem slightly more considerate.

DO YOU SIT ON PUBLIC TOILETS?

We mean, of course, without lining it with toilet tissue or that sanitary Saran Wrap–like skin. A third of us (more women than men but not overwhelmingly) would rather eat snakes than sit on an unknown unprotected seat. Some 33.9 percent led by southerners (42.7 percent) and northeasterners (39.7 percent) *never* sit on a public throne. Then there's the 12.3 percent of the population who wouldn't give it a second thought.

WHICH STALL DO YOU CHOOSE?

Assuming they're all spotless, of course, we rarely choose the first *or* last when there are many options—like at an airport. The folks who stock the toilet tissue in public johns can confirm that when given two stalls, Americans seem to prefer the one on their right. But when there are three, all of them get pretty much the same usage with the middle receiving slightly more business.

GIVEN A CHOICE, DO YOU USE THE HANDICAPPED STALL?

More than half of us (55 percent) would do so only when the others are occupied because the seat is too high. Twenty percent say it makes absolutely no difference. Another 25 percent prefer it because it's roomier.

WHAT DO YOU DO IF THERE'S NO TOILET PAPER?

To ward off this veritable crisis, many of us (42 percent) check before committing to the stall and if there's no paper we go elsewhere—or hold it. One in five of us carries tissues in our purse or pockets for just such an emergency. The same number of people would summon the courage to ask next door (16 percent) as would drip dry, air dry, or shake it off. Many punters would scream and curse. Others would improvise with coarser napkins or paper towels—even the crinkly paper wrapping the toilet roll came in or, in a real pinch, the cardboard spool. One intrepid respondent said if no one was around she'd sneak into another stall.

DO YOU GO TO THE TOILET ON A SCHEDULE?

Twelve percent of us claim we eliminate by the clock. On the other hand, almost 20 percent of us can't immediately recall when we went last. Most of us *are* on some sort of schedule, though it's hardly rigid. The average person visits the john five to six times a day.

DO YOU RUN THE WATER FAUCET TO DISGUISE THE SOUND OF PEE?

More than one of every six of us turns on the tap to camouflage the sound of tinkle. Single folks are twice as conscientious as marrieds and younger people more concerned than olders.

DO YOU ALWAYS WASH YOUR HANDS AFTER GOING TO THE BATHROOM?

Mothers of America take pride: you (and the warning signs in all the bathrooms in Chinese restaurants) have trained your children well. More than half (54.2 percent) wash with soap and water all the time. A fourth of us just rinse with water. Less than 2 percent *admit* they never wash their hands after going.

DO YOU ALWAYS FLUSH?

"When it's yellow let it mellow, when it's brown flush it down." That's the motto almost one in every four of us lives by. Some 23.5 percent of us *admit* we don't *always* flush, though richer people and midwesterners are pretty close to sainthood here.

DO YOU FLUSH WHILE YOU'RE SITTING DOWN?

A third of us stay seated through the process while two-thirds stand up before finishing their business.

IN A PUBLIC JOHN, WHAT DO YOU USE TO FLUSH?

In the East, the sole or heel of the shoe is the preferred method. More than half of us limber up and contort to depress the flush with our footwear. Westerners and midwesterners tend to use their hands and southerners wrap toilet tissue around to ward off germs and condensation—or worse.

WE KNOW YOU PEE IN THE JOHN . . . BUT WHERE ELSE?

There's a joke going round to define a schmuck—it's the guy who gets out of the shower to take a pee. Americans seem to have taken that homily to heart. Almost half of us—45.2 percent—pee in the shower, more even than those (44.9 percent) who urinate in the ocean. Watch out for those young single men: they're least discriminatory about where to go. We're a *bit* more reticent in a pool, but no need to hold the chlorine: 28.1 percent of us admit we pee there. Amazingly, midwesterners, the most prissy of any region when it comes to letting go in the ocean, are loosest of all about peeing in a pool. Almost one in three of us does, with younger folks almost twice as likely as olders.

WHAT, OTHER THAN USE "THE FACILITIES," DO YOU DO IN THE THRONE ROOM?

Four out of 10 of us read there and one out of five smoke. Fourteen percent say they listen to the radio and 8 percent chat on the phone.

DO YOU LET FIDO WATCH YOU PEE?

Fido can watch the whole procedure as far as 57.1 percent say. There's no age or geographic disparity precluding pets from entering the bathroom when their owners are using the facilities.

DO YOU USE THE TOILET WITH THE DOOR OPEN?

Who could have imagined how loosey-goosey America is? More than half of us—53.9 percent—sometimes pee with the door open and another 7.7 percent always do—though poorer people are twice as likely as the rich to keep an open-door policy always and northeasterners more than twice as prone as westerners. A third of us—38.1 percent—wouldn't dream of ever leaving the door open.

DO YOU LET SOMEONE ELSE IN THE BATHROOM WHILE USING THE TOILET?

Alas, the last private domain of America has been invaded. More than half of us—55.2 percent—let someone else in the bathroom while they go. Interestingly, married or not doesn't seem to make much difference.

WHEN YOU USE THE TOILET IN THE MIDDLE OF THE NIGHT, DO YOU USUALLY TURN ON THE LIGHT?

Maybe younger people are afraid of the dark but they're considerably (okay, 12 percent) more likely to flip on the light switch. Married folks, perhaps because they know the way and their steps are well trodden, are less likely than singles. And women (is it confidence or consideration?) seem pretty content to pee in the dark.

WHAT DO YOU DO WHEN YOU'RE WEARING A BATHING SUIT AND HAVE TO PEE?

Astonishingly, two-thirds of women remove the whole she-bang. Just a third slide the bottom flap to one side.

DO YOU PEEK IN YOUR HOST'S BATHROOM CABINET?

Almost four out of 10 (39 percent) can't resist their curiosity, while 60 percent say they do not snoop—and would not. (Singles and divorced folks are almost twice as likely as marrieds to give in to this temptation, and younger folks more inclined than their elders.) Some 77 percent were disappointed: they could find nothing unusual in the cabinets. But others have spotted a dead rodent, a toupee, a glass eye, and a gun.

Amazingly, hosts must anticipate loo lookers because 38 percent say they remove personal items before guests arrive. And 17 percent of those who snuck glances into their hosts bathroom admit they've been caught. How do you get out of that one?

HAVE YOU EVERY USED A HOST'S TOOTHBRUSH, COMB, OR MAKEUP WITHOUT ASKING?

One out of four of us admits it, yet 36 percent of people in the central states fess up. Men are likelier than women (29 percent to 21 percent) to use someone else's personal items.

WHAT'S YOUR TOILET PAPER OF CHOICE?

More than four out of five (85 percent) of Americans want two-ply toilet tissue. Just 20 percent prefer a color other than white though 18- to 25-year-olds (32 percent) are more likely to opt for pink or blue. Just around half (48 percent) like their toilet paper quilted and 44 percent opt for a decorative box instead of a plain box.

COMPANY'S COMING: DO YOU CHANGE THE ROLL?

Almost nine out of 10 of us (88 percent) figure if it's good enough for the family, it's good enough for guests. But women by a 15 percent to 9 percent margin are more inclined to insert a different though not always plushier roll for company. Among those who do switch brands for company, 70 percent replace the everyday paper with a costlier one while 15 percent put out the cheaper stuff.

STUCK WITH AN EMPTY ROLL?

It's happened to three out of four of us, and to 22 percent of us it seems to happen more than once a month. But here's a benefit of bachelorhood: 53 percent of live-alones say it *never* happens to them.

WHAT'S YOUR FAVORITE BATHROOM COLOR?

Blue is America's favorite bathroom hue, cited by 22 percent of respondents, followed by white (13 percent) and green, 11 percent. And while pink and black are the favored shades for 8 percent of the population each, 15 percent cite black as their least favorite color and 11 percent shudder at the thought of pink.

DO YOU BIDET?

Bidets may be as common as faucets in France but three out of four Americans have never used one—and 14 percent aren't sure what it is. Less than 1 percent of American households have one.

DO YOU USE ONE SWAB FOR BOTH EARS?

Not if there are two available. Some 59 percent would use a separate swab for each ear while 21 percent would dig in with one for both. Eleven percent say they don't use cotton swabs to clean their ears. Maybe that's because they've got bobby pins, pinkies, and car keys handy.

MANNERS

When it comes to manners, there are some big surprises. Fewer than three of every four of us think being polite is really important and even less regard good table manners as something to strive for.

DO YOU SWEAR?

You're ---n right we do—an average of 16 times a day. That number drops if we have kids. Approximately one in 10 of us thinks he or she swears too much.

DO YOU EVER SPIT?

Three out of every five of us have from time to time been known to expurgate on public streets, with men almost twice as likely as women to do so. Singles, young folks, the less wealthy, and surprisingly, midwesterners spit more than the average.

IS THAT A CARROT ON YOUR ENAMEL OR DO YOU JUST HAVE ORANGE TEETH?

When it comes to bluntness, we have our peculiarities. We'd sooner tell someone that his fly was down than that he had broccoli stuck in his teeth. More than four out of five of us— 81.3 percent—would tell an acquaintance to zip up, while just

69 percent would alert them to vegetable bits edged in their chompers. Maybe it's a male bonding thing, but men almost always tell their buddies as well as total strangers. Women, on the other hand, would tell close friends, but only a third would alert a stranger. Three out of four women—77 percent—would point out a smudge on someone's face but just 14 percent would point out dandruff.

IS THAT A WEAPON IN YOUR POCKET OR . . .

It hardly seems civil but almost every seventh person in America carries a weapon. The most likely: a knife or gun. Two-thirds think physical force is often justified. Sixty percent have used physical violence against another. Fewer than half regret their action.

DO YOU ACKNOWLEDGE A SNEEZE?

Few out there seem to go to great lengths on this one. One in five men remain paralyzingly mute. Another 15 percent mutter Gesundheit; that's more than twice the women who do so. But significantly more women than men say, "God bless you." Others routinely rebuke the sneezer with an "Excuse you," "Pardon you," "Cover your mouth," or "Slow down."

HAVE YOU EVER APPLIED LIPSTICK AT A RESTAURANT TABLE?

Oops. Some 17 percent shamefacedly admit that they do apply it at a table in a restaurant. Richer women are five times as guilty as less affluent ones.

HOW OFTEN DO YOU IGNORE RSVP?

Most of us know just what RSVP means but almost a third of us—29 percent and considerably higher among northeasterners—confess that within the last three months they've failed to let someone know their intentions. Most miscreants make some excuse if called by the would-be host, but more often it's a "I-never-received-the-invitation" sort of thing rather than a confession to their own breach of conduct. We feel much less guilt if it's a business event.

WHAT DO YOU DO WITH TESTER STRIPS AND MAGAZINE SUBSCRIPTION OFFERS THAT TUMBLE OUT OF MAGAZINES?

An overwhelming majority—93 percent of us—throw them out in a huff. Others are more inventive—though rarely as resourceful as Martha Stewart retiling the pool with discarded plastic credit cards. A few of us use them as bookmarks. Some mail them back to the company so it pays the postage.

DO YOU GIVE UP YOUR SEAT ON A BUS OR TRAIN FOR SOMEONE NEEDIER?

There is a shred of decency, kindness, and courtesy in America. Almost three-fourths of us, 72 percent, say we usually give up our seats on the bus or train for a pregnant or elderly person. Almost one in five of us—18 percent—claim they never have the opportunity: they don't use public transportation.

HOW ABOUT GETTING OFF THE ELEVATOR?

Most men—84 percent,—say they typically step back to allow women to get off the elevator before them. But perhaps, as one cynic suggests, "they're doing it to eye women's bodies." Older men are slightly more gracious than middle-agers who are slightly more gracious than young men. Marrieds are considerably more gentlemanly than singles and small-towners put suburban and rural men to shame.

... OPENING THE CAR DOOR FOR THE OPPOSITE SEX?

Though it may be a lightning rod of sexual egalitarianism, seven out of 10 men say they open the car door for a lady. Most—77 percent—are older "gentlemen" who learned at their mom's knee and smaller towners.

GUM CHEWERS, HOW DO YOU USUALLY DISPOSE OF THE FLAVORLESS GLOB?

Are these survey respondents going to the same movie theaters the rest of us frequent? Only 7.4 percent confess they sometimes stick their remnant on furniture—including under desks, tables, and, of course, the bottom of theater seats. Watch out for the young ones—they're almost seven times as likely as older folks to plant their used gum there. For the most part, gum chewers are law abiding. Half profess to wrap their leftover sticks in a piece of paper and discard; 16 percent just toss it in the street. Sixteen of every 100 of us never chew gum. More than a third of us feel people shouldn't chew gum in public.

HOW ABOUT THOSE TOENAIL CLIPPINGS?

We're a lot more conscientious about how we dispose of our toenail clippings than we are about our gum—or boogies. More than six out of 10 of us claim we carefully scoop them up and deposit them in the trash can but more than one in four lets them lie where they fall. Again, it's the younguns who are three times likelier than the old ones who are the slobs. Then again, six percent of us never clip our toenails.

HOW DO YOU DEAL WITH AN AD BEFORE THE MOVIE?

Used to be lots of hissing and booing. Now there's essentially bored indifference. Screenvision Cinema Network, the nation's only cinema advertising company, says 96 percent of patrons approve of advertising trailers. We couldn't find them. Less than half of us feel anything short of cynical about "these ads we pay for," and most of us respond by paying no attention, shifting uncomfortably in our seats, getting up for the popcorn, or talking through them.

WHAT DO YOU DO WHEN PEOPLE AROUND YOU TALK DURING A MOVIE?

A third of Americans and almost half of all midwesterners do absolutely nothing: they let the yakkers yak. But don't mess with a westerner's movie rights. They're twice as likely—40 percent—to whisper "shh" to hush the annoying babble than to let it go.

DO YOU CUT LONG LINES OR WAIT PATIENTLY?

Three-quarters of us will wait, but probably impatiently. Only a fourth will cut in line; in this virtueless group is a disproportionate number of men and northeasterners.

WHAT WOULD YOU DO TO SOMEONE WHO CUTS THE LINE?

Just about seven out of 10 of us—male and female alike—would protest, with men slightly more than women—76 versus 65 percent—taking the offensive.

DO YOU SPY?

You bet you do, you nosy folks. A third of us—32.3 percent—sometimes or always steal a glance at other people's mail. Almost half of us—45.8 percent—sometimes or always read documents that don't relate to us at work. And more than seven out of 10 of us—71.6 percent—say we eavesdrop.

WOULD YOU READ THE DIARY OF SOMEONE CLOSE ENOUGH YOU'RE BOUND TO BE IN IT?

A medicine cabinet is one thing but someone's personal—perhaps locked—diary? Half of us could not resist the urge. Women are slightly more curious—54 to 47 percent—than men about seeing how they play out in their significant other's mind.

HOW MANY TIMES A DAY DO YOU THINK YOU BELCH?

Men burp 4.7 times a day, while women burp 2.1 times a day. Midwesterners belch 4.06 times a day; northeasterners only burp 2.6 times a day.

WHAT DO YOU DO IF YOU CAN'T SUPPRESS A FART OR BELCH?

A third of us—35.2 percent—would let it rip. Men, westerners, and southpaws are significantly more inclined to let go than women. Some 19 percent of us would go to another room, preferably the bathroom, and 11.6 of us would do the deed and then apologize. One in 10 of us would try to squelch it until later. Many people refused to say what they'd do.

DO YOU EVER TRY TO SAVE AN EXTRA SEAT FOR YOURSELF, SAY, ON A TRAIN? WHAT'S YOUR STRATEGY?

More than three of every four of us—77.1 percent—has resorted to some dodge to save a seat. The most common strategy adopted by 44.9 percent of us is to cover the seat with a coat or other sprawling item. Some 10.6 percent of us have fibbed, claiming we're saving the seat for someone. Some 6.8 percent avoid eye contact and 5.5 percent of us have actually faked being asleep—stretched out or too closely bordering the seat for someone to take it comfortably. Another 3.2 percent say they glare at potential seatmates to ward them off. Amazingly, midwesterners are four times as likely as northeasterners to take such a hostile stance.

HOW DO YOU DEAL WITH UNWANTED CALLS?

Ice cream is dribbling from the supermarket bag, the groceries are unpacking themselves and the phone rings; the caller launches into a singsong spiel about a worthy product or cause to get you to part with your dollars. Astonishingly, almost one of every four of us hears the caller out. But not westerners. When it comes to telemarketers, they're an impatient lot; northeasterners are more than twice as likely to listen to the pitch. More than one in four of us—26.8 percent—just hang up, and almost half—45.5 percent—politely interrupt and cut the caller off. Another 12.6 percent worry about hurting the caller's feelings and make up some excuse to ring off.

WHAT DO YOU DO WHEN SOMEONE ASKS HOW MUCH YOU'VE PAID FOR SOMETHING?

Though we've been taught it's rude to ask, three out of five of us—59.7 percent—tell the truth. Just one in 10 of us though—three times as many northeasterners as westerners—would say it's none of your business. An equal number would ignore them or feign ignorance. One in 10 of us—with midwesterners four times as likely as northeasterners—would outright lie.

DO YOU ASK BEFORE TAKING THE LAST HELPING OF FOOD, OR JUST GO FOR IT?

Admittedly, a different set of manners applies at someone else's house than at our own homes, but *chez nous* just 44 percent of us ask before grabbing the last helping of stuffing or slice of peach pie. In "family style" servings at restaurants slightly less than one out of four just goes for it, and at others' homes almost everyone asks.

DO YOU BELIEVE IN THE CLEAN PLATE AWARD OR DO YOU REGULARLY LEAVE SOMETHING BEHIND?

Wasn't everyone taught as a child that it's proper to leave a pea or string bean behind? More than half of us—56 percent—say we rarely leave a morsel behind, though a few say it depends on how hungry we are. Some 44 percent try to leave something behind. One respondent who'd been browbeaten as a child to finish everything served said it took years of therapy but now she can leave something on the plate.

DO YOU EVER SEND FOOD BACK IN A RESTAURANT?

No matter that the steak is well done and you ordered rare, more than a third of us—34.2 percent—never send food back to the kitchen. Three of every five of us—59.4 percent—appear to have had some assertiveness training. And 5.5 percent of us are a waiter's nightmare. Watch out for young western men: they seem quickest to return food to the kitchen.

DO YOU EVER TAKE HOME LEFTOVERS?

Though one in 10 of us claim we've never toted home a doggy bag almost one in four of us—22.6 percent—does all the time. Women are likelier than men.

DO YOU EVER STIFF THE WAITER FOR POOR SERVICE?

Half of us—50.3 percent—would never dream of withholding a tip no matter how rotten the service. The rest of us—especially men—would factor in circumstances, including the malicious intent of the server, in deciding how to retaliate.

The likeliest way is by reducing the tip (not eliminating it). Some 87 percent of us would cut it back significantly. (Another 93 percent would increase the *pourboire* to reward excellent service.) Some 43 percent of us claim to have walked out of a restaurant because of bad service—most before the entree was served. And many of us have bad-mouthed the perpetrator. MasterCard International found restaurant goers who've had a bad experience will warn off an average of five people. But if they've had a great meal, they'll tell six.

IF SEATED NEXT TO THE LOO OR SWINGING KITCHEN DOORS WOULD YOU ASK TO CHANGE TABLES?

Under dire circumstances—like next to a cigar smoker—two-thirds of us would summon the courage. But 34.8 percent of us are just too cowed. Older folks are 10 percent more likely than under 35s to speak up and you could just about blow the exhaust fan in a midwesterner's face to elicit the request: 50.7 percent would *never* ask to change tables.

WOULD YOU ASK ANOTHER PATRON NOT TO SMOKE?

Again, midwesterners have more tolerance than the rest of us. Even if the smoke were getting in their eyes, four out of five would never risk offending someone. Indeed, 71.3 percent of the population would inhale and bear it. Just 28.3 percent of people would always or sometimes address the issue.

MONEY AND SMART STUFF

IF YOU CAN REED THIS BOOK, MEYBE YOU'RE IN THE OTHER HAF.

Some 22 percent of us are functionally illiterate—including many high school graduates. Nearly half of our 191 million adults aren't proficient enough in English to compose a letter about a billing error or to figure out the length of a bus trip from a published schedule.

HOW MUCH TIME DO YOU SPEND READING?

All told, labels, traffic signs, lottery tickets, the average Jane spends 164 minutes a day reading, while the average Joe reads for 150 minutes a day. As for intentional reading of books, newspapers, and magazines, middle-agers spend only 2.8 hours a week whereas retirees log 6 to 7 hours a week. Some 28 percent of us haven't read even one book in the last six months.

IS USING CORRECT GRAMMAR IMPORTANT?

Less than half of us—45 percent—rank it as something worth striving for. And that's even before the schools began teaching whole language and invented spelling.

DO YOU SPEAK A SECOND LANGUAGE?

Seven out of 10 of us say it's hard enough mastering one language yet alone adding a foreign tongue. Fewer than one in 10 of us speaks three languages or more.

IS THAT 12 FLASHING ON YOUR VCR?

More than a third of us—37 percent—claim to know how to use all the features on a VCR. Roughly the same number admit they wouldn't have a clue how to fix the telltale flash.

CAN YOU WORK THE MICROWAVE?

More than half of us—58 percent—have (finally) figured out all the settings on their microwave.

DO YOU USE AN ATM?

Again, more than half of us—53 percent—are quite comfortable using a bank automated teller machine. Some 46 percent actually prefer it to a live person. Almost two out of three households—62 percent—with an annual income over $40,000 use them versus 20 percent with incomes under $20,000.

ARE YOU COMFORTABLE FIGURING OUT THE TIP?

Less than a third of us say we feel competent figuring out the tip even when it comes to captains and wine stewards. Men, perhaps because of practice, claim to be slightly more adept at it at 30 versus 25 percent.

CAN YOU NAVIGATE THE INFORMATION SUPERHIGHWAY?

More than one of every 10 of us—11 percent—claims he or she is charging down the technopath in fifth gear. A third—33 percent—figure they're "going the speed limit in the right lane." Only one out of 10 of us admits to techno-illiteracy, that we're either stalled or going the wrong way in cyberspace.

WHAT'S THE SMALLEST AMOUNT OF MONEY THAT YOU'D STOP TO PICK UP OFF THE STREET?

If the streets were lined with gold, not copper, maybe we'd be more prone to bend. Almost half of us—46.1 percent—would see a penny lying there and walk on by. Some 13.9 percent would stoop for a nickel, another 7.4 percent wouldn't bother with anything less than a dime, and for 15.2 percent it has to be worth 25 cents to stop. Astonishingly, 8.4 percent of people—and 11.8 percent of those under 35—wouldn't pick up anything short of a dollar. Talk about the value of money.

DO YOU SAVE OLD PENNIES?

We won't stop on the street to pick up pennies but more than half of us—52 percent—say we have stashes of them on window sills, bookshelves, and other out of the way places. Banks used to supply rollers free; now they charge for taking them off our hands.

DO YOU KNOW WHAT THE DOW JONES INDUSTRIAL AVERAGE MEANS?

More than four out of five of us have a foggy notion but fewer than one in five (19 percent) know it refers to the combined price of the stock of 30 major corporations on any day. Most people think it refers to the average price of "Dow Jones stock" on any day.

DO YOU PLAY SWEEPSTAKES?

Fewer than one in 20 of us who receive a sweepstakes pitch in the mail actually responds to it. Players tend to come from all regions and income levels: they just have a gambling twitch.

DO YOU KNOW WHAT DRY BEER MEANS?

For all the advertising devoted to defining it, fewer than half of us know it means a brew that's less sweet. Not surprisingly, men are better versed in beer lore than women.

HOW ABOUT IMPORT QUOTAS?

Two-thirds of us—64 percent—haven't got the vaguest idea what import quotas mean. And of the 36 percent who claim to have some inkling, few would stake their life on defining it accurately.

WHO DOES THE CHECKBOOK?

In married or cohabitative households where finances are pooled, three out of five women say they're solely responsible for balancing the checkbook. And more than half—56 percent—are solely responsible for paying bills. As for developing a family budget? More than a third—38 percent—say they're captain.

DO YOU KNOW HOW MUCH YOUR SPOUSE MAKES?

Three out of 10 wives and husbands are in the dark. What we make is apparently the last taboo. Our collective shyness or secretiveness about finances extends to other family members. Just 26 percent of moms and 19 percent of dads know how much their kids earn and 19 percent of children know what their parents make. We'd rather talk about a friend's marital problems (55 to 47 percent) than shaky finances.

WOULD YOU SELL YOUR SPOUSE FOR A MILLION?

Two out of three of us, holding tight to those holy vows, wouldn't lend their spouse for a night, even for a million bucks. One in 10 would accept this indecent proposal while 16 percent admit they'd mull it over. Another 13 percent aren't talking.

WHAT WORRIES YOU MORE, YOUR FINANCIAL OR PHYSICAL SECURITY?

You can talk about crime but five times as many people worry more about their financial security than about their physical safety. Eighty-three percent fret about money while just 15 percent are concerned about harm coming to them.

WHAT'S YOUR BIGGEST MONEY WORRY?

One in four of us—26 percent—gets chills thinking about being audited by the IRS. Only 7 percent have actually ever had the pleasure. Fourteen percent are frightened by the prospect of doing their own taxes and 11 percent dread the thought of having a credit card declined in public. A fourth of us—27 percent—have bounced a check, 23 percent have been contacted by a collection agent for a late bill, 2 percent have filed for bankruptcy, and 4 percent have been the victim of a financial scam.

EVER BOUGHT A PROGRAM THAT PROMISED TO MAKE YOU RICH?

Fewer than one in 100 actually has subscribed to the bevy of offers for programs that will make us productive and economically savvy, but almost one in 10 at least fleetingly has contemplated it. Most didn't follow through because they didn't think the program would work. Others say they were too costly. Still others simply procrastinated.

DO YOU BELIEVE IN HORATIO ALGER?

Over half of us—59 percent—believe that with elbow grease you can succeed. Two percent feel it takes a cutthroat ruthlessness and 14 percent think you just have to be lucky. Twelve percent believe the road to riches is paved with family wealth.

IS NEVER PAY RETAIL YOUR ELEVENTH COMMANDMENT?

Half of us—54 percent—perhaps inspired by the Ben Franklin eulogy to thrift, admit we always look for a bargain. Roughly three out of five shoppers routinely check prices and 41 percent figure their worst financial gaffe was having overpaid for something. Almost half—46 percent—claim they're very disciplined about money and 19 percent say they're "very tight" with it.

CAN YOU TELL IF THE PRICE IS RIGHT?

Slightly less than half of us can correctly guess the price of items we often buy within 15 seconds of putting them in our grocery carts.

Personality Stuff

NOT THAT YOU'D EVER PROVOKE ONE, OF COURSE, BUT JUST SAY IT HAPPENED: HOW DO YOU THINK YOU'D FARE IN A FISTFIGHT?

More than half of men—54 percent—figure they'd do better than average. So do 24 percent of women. Who ever said testesterone didn't equate to positive thinking?

DO YOU KEEP A GUN AT HOME?

Nearly two of every five families with children—37 percent—keep a firearm in the house. More than one in four handgun owners—27 percent—keeps the guns loaded; more than half (51 percent) store them unlocked.

EVER TAKEN MUSIC LESSONS?

Only four of every 10 of us have ever taken lessons for an instrument. Piano is the top choice followed by guitar. A decade ago, 47 percent of us had taken lessons.

HAVE YOU EVER PLAYED IN A BAND?

At some point in their lives, one out of five Americans has.

STUDIED ART?

Fewer than one in five—18 percent—has ever taken lessons in visual arts but 23 percent of us have taken an art appreciation class. More than one in four of us—27 percent—has gone to a museum or art gallery at least once in the last year. Forty-one percent have attended an arts and crafts fair.

DO YOU USUALLY READ THE LAST PAGE OF THE BOOK FIRST?

Some 15.8 percent of us can't wait and read the last page, with women almost four times likelier than men to do so. Some 27.7 percent skip pages to find out what's going to happen— again with women almost twice as likely to do so.

DO YOU ALWAYS FINISH THE BOOK?

Almost half of us—43.5 percent—always finish a book once we start it. Young folks are more than twice as likely as middle-agers to abandon reading matter they find uninteresting.

WHEN READING A BOOK HOW DO YOU MARK YOUR PLACE?

There are two kinds of people in the world, those who fold down the page and those who use a bookmark. The courteous sort who treat books with respect and don't deface property edge out the for-my-convenience page-folders 42.9 percent to 39.7 percent. Then there are those who use the flap of a hardcover—8.4 percent—and those who don't mark the page at all (8.4 percent).

SNAKES OR SPIDERS

More of us—33 percent—are ophidiophobics than arachnophopidics—that is, we're more scared stiff of snakes than we are of spiders and other creepy crawlers. But on the index of what scares us out of our wits, it's making a speech, getting fat, or having to hang around high or exposed places or the dentist's chair. More than half of us are terrified by these prospects. Just about a third of us also have a major fear of flying. Eight percent of us are also unnerved by thunder and lightning, 4 percent by crowds and dogs, 2 percent by cats, and 3 percent by the prospect of driving a car or even going out of the house.

WHAT'S YOUR FAVORITE COLOR?

More of us pick blue than any other hue. Next comes red, followed by green, white, pink, purple, orange, and yellow. Poorer people tend to prefer simple colors that can be described in two words—"grass green" or "sky blue," for instance. Richer folks opt for complex colors that require three or more words for an accurate description—like "grey green with a hint of blue." Forest green and burgundy are favored by the wealthier 3 percent of Americans.

DO YOU REUSE THE TINFOIL?

It's not just a Howard Hughes thing but rich people, even more than poor, tend to smooth the tinfoil to reuse. Some 44 percent of people say they try to get more than one use out of aluminum foil with midwesterners, southerners, and young people more likely than the rest of us. (The latter claim it's the ecological thing to do.)

WHAT ABOUT WRAPPING PAPER?

Again, ecology has made reusing gift wrap a status badge. Some 57 percent of people say they save pretty gift paper that's in good condition along with bows and boxes to recycle.

DO YOU GIVE GIFTS AWAY THAT HAVE BEEN GIVEN TO YOU?

Nancy Reagan took a lot of heat for sending her grandchild the stuffed bear he'd left at the White House on his last visit as a birthday present, but the practice is *a lot* more common than the censure the then First Lady took suggests. More than half of us admit we occasionally pass off as purchased for the occasion a tidbit that's been given to us. In fact, common knowledge has it that there are just a dozen fruitcakes in the world—passing from one gift basket to another.

DO YOU COLLECT RUBBER BANDS?

What else can you do with them? Fewer than a third of us say we throw them out as soon as these elastic bands find their way into our homes. The rest wait until rubber band fortresses have emerged or make concerted efforts to find other ways to use them.

HAVE YOU EVER CRIED AT WORK?

Even when served the big pink slip, men manage to keep a stiff upper lip. Less than one in five says he's ever cried at work but just about three of every five women have been sob sisters. This despite the fact that 75 percent of both sexes feel work is not the place to break down or to let their emotions show.

DO YOU WHISTLE WHILE YOU WORK?

It may have worked for the seven dwarves but we are not as happy-go-lucky a nation as you might think. Just one in five of us—19 percent—often whistles, sings, or hums while we work.

CHAMPAGNE, CREDIT CARD, OR ROLODEX?

When you're feeling blue and need a pick-me-up, what do you do? More people reach out and touch someone—over fiber optics, that is—than break out the champagne or credit card for a shopping expedition. Some 34 percent of us dial to indulge, with women representing 41 percent of those and men 26 percent. College grads and older folks are likeliest to phone (42 and 41 percent, respectively) while young folks are likelier to try something else.

HAVE YOU BAKED FROM A MIX AND TRIED TO PASS IT OFF AS SCRATCH?

Let's call it fudging—a sin of omission rather than commission. More than three out of five of us—66 percent of women and 59 percent of men—admit they've used a mix to whip up cakes, cookies, brownies, or muffins within the last year—and taken credit for producing the home-baked treat. Roughly half say they have admitted—or would admit—they got some help if asked. The rest have thrown away the telltale box, changed the subject, or outright fibbed.

HOW ABOUT LAUGHS?

More than half of us—56 percent—(between guffaws) claim that we laugh more than most people. Two out of five of us feel happy often and 28 percent look forward to each new day. Just one in 10 of us—9 percent—thinks of himself or herself as a curmudgeon who is frequently angry.

IS THE GLASS HALF-FULL OR HALF-EMPTY?

Some 46 percent of men and 52 percent of women describe themselves as optimists while 8 percent of men and 11 percent of women see themselves as pessimists. (The rest say they're neither.) People 35 to 44 years are most likely to see the glass as half-full—56 percent—while only 11 percent of those over 45s see it that way.

ARE YOU A HOROSCOPE JUNKIE?

"What's your sign?" may no longer be a standard conversational opener but our astrological heritage is more familiar to many of us than our social security number. Roughly one in 10 of us admits we seek out astrological advice in newspapers and magazines and more than half—53 percent—can't resist checking their horoscope when flipping past it in print.

HOW FORGETFUL ARE YOU?

Not totally amnesiac, but close. Fully 16 percent of us have forgotten our wedding anniversaries, with 22 percent of men versus 11 percent of women guilty as charged. Westerners had the greatest memory lapse: 22 percent forgot the big day while only 12 percent of northeasterners did. Newlyweds, those married five years or less, were slightly less forgetful than old-timers—13 versus 16 percent. And those making $15,000 or less a year were the least likely to forget. Just 10 percent did.

BORROWER OR LENDER BE?

We seem to have ignored Polonius's words of advice to Hamlet—"neither a borrower nor lender be." Just 35 percent of us claim we never borrow anything—other than library books. Some 37 percent of men say they've borrowed others' tools while a fourth of women borrow sugar, or eggs (22 percent), coffee (5 percent), and ice (3 percent.)

WHAT WOULD IT TAKE TO GET YOU TO TAKE A CAB?

For a third of us, nothing could do the trick: we never take cabs. But another 10 percent would hail one (admittedly in bad weather) for fewer than five blocks. Twice as many men as women would take a cab for less than two blocks. Interestingly, those with the least stamina (or greater desire for comfort) tend to be those least able to afford it.

EVER BEEN AUDITED?

More than four of every five of us admits we've taken at least as much as we could on their tax forms but fewer than one in five has had at least correspondence with the Internal Revenue Service. The IRS says it audits 1 percent of the population a year. People who earn more than $100,000 are the most likely to hear from the tax man.

DO YOU REGULARLY CHECK YOURSELF OUT IN STORE WINDOWS AND MIRRORS?

Narcissus would be proud. We're clearly a nation of folks who revel in our own reflections. Almost a fourth of us—22.3 percent—steal glances of ourselves all the time with women, young folks, and singles more prone to do so. Another two-thirds—68.7 percent—admit to doing so sometimes. Only 9 percent say they're oblivious.

HOW DO YOU STACK UP IN THE MIRROR?

It seems, however, that all that glance stealing may not be making us smile. Few of us think we're the fairest of them all. In fact, most of us—59 percent—see ourselves as average-looking. Only 5 percent of us describe ourselves as handsome or beautiful, 1 percent as unattractive, and 31 percent as above average. Blacks are more than twice as likely as whites to call themselves beautiful, and college grads 14 percent more likely to call themselves above average.

HOW ABOUT ON THE PERSONALITY ODOMETER?

Looks, of course, hardly measure anything, people *say*. Kindness, they tell us, is a more pressing criteria. Almost half of us—45 percent—see ourselves as above average in kindness. Some 42 percent of us consider ourselves funny. A third of us—34 percent—see ourselves as being more patient than most and 32 percent admit we're more ambitious. A fourth of us—27 percent—consider ourselves smarter than the masses. The rich and influential have more rose-colored glasses. They see themselves as possessing far more virtues than the rest of the population.

WHAT'S YOUR FAVORITE ROOM?

The old adage, "No matter where I serve my guests they seem to like my kitchen best" apparently rings true. Some 46 percent of women and 26 percent of men like to hang out best near the stove.

WHEN THE PRESSURE'S ON WHERE DO YOU TURN?

Three out of four of us turn on the TV. More than a third of us—38 percent—prefer to vent with a good scream at some-one. Two-thirds of us blow off steam by listening to music and 61 percent find solace in a bath or shower. More than half of us—57 percent—go for a walk to bust stress. Women are twice as likely to shop it off—54 versus 27 percent—as men, and three times as likely to clean house—55 versus 20 percent. Men are more inclined to exercise—41 versus 36 percent. Only 22 percent of men and women say they hit the bottle to reduce stress. A third have sex.

WHERE ARE YOU WATCHING?

More of that eerie blue light emanates from the living room and/or den than anywhere else—67 percent of all our TV watching is done there. But it's hardly the only place, for sure. One percent of our viewing is done in basements, 19 percent in bedrooms, 2 percent in the kitchen, and less than 1 percent in the garage, bathroom, and assorted closets.

DO YOU CONSIDER YOURSELF A COUCH POTATO?

We may not like the phrase *couch potato* but a rose by any other name would smell the same—that is, well baked. Some 38 percent of men and 29 percent of women say lying down watching TV is a regular pastime, though 68 percent of us would prefer to call ourselves *homebodies.*

ARE YOU WATCHING WITH BATED BREATH?

In the average home TVs and radios are on 11 hours a day. More than half of us—58 percent of men and 57 percent of women—say we're satisfied with what's on. Blacks are more content than whites—75 versus 55 percent—and 13- to 17-year-olds are more satisfied—75 percent—than any other age group. Older folks are the most malcontent. Only 52 percent of those 50 or over claim to be satisfied.

IS THAT WANDERLUST OR A JOB RELOCATION?

We seem to be a fairly restless lot. One in five of us picked up and moved last year. On average, we move 11 times in our lifetimes. Young people have especially restless feet. Almost a fourth of those 18 to 24 have pulled up stakes and plopped down elsewhere, while just 7 percent of middle agers have done so. Some 61 percent of us live in the state where we were born.

THE VISA BILL OR MOUNT HELENAS ERUPTING?

Two out of five of us describe ourselves as worriers. For 15 percent of us, it's bills keeping us awake at night. Just 2 percent fret about a natural disaster.

DO YOU USE AN ALARM CLOCK?

Few of us have built-in time sensors. Of the 90 percent who need a jolt, roughly half have their alarm clocks set to music or to a buzzer, and just 5 percent to news.

DO YOU TAKE THE ADVICE COLUMNISTS AS GOSPEL?

Some 53 percent of us put our faith in the Anne Landers of the world. Women are far likelier than men to follow advice columnists; almost two in every three pore over them. Middle incomers and over 50s are likelier than baby boomers or younger and rich or poor folks, as are Democrats, more so than Republicans, political moderates more so than liberals or conservatives, and oddly, white Protestants and evangelicalists more so than other religious groups.

DO YOU SET YOUR WATCH AHEAD?

They may take a lickin' and keep on tickin' but they certainly don't tell the time in shall we say real time? Just one-third of us—32 percent—don't play time games with ourselves. The most common leap forward is five minutes—some 34 percent of us adjust our watches ahead that much—but 8 percent set it ahead around 10 minutes, and 6 percent by 15 minutes. Sixteen percent of us move it ahead—but aren't sure by how much. That's part of the impetus to get there on time, they say. Fewer westerners juggle time, but when they do it's often in big increments. Four percent of us don't wear a watch at all.

DO YOU LOCK YOUR FRONT DOOR?

Crime has made us wary. Six out of 10 of us wouldn't go to the mailbox without guarding the fortress. Interestingly, women are more than 12 percent more relaxed than men on this front. Midwesterners have also let down their guards. Some 12 percent—four times the number of westerners—never lock the door.

DO YOU TURN ON THE LIGHTS AT NIGHT WHEN YOU GO OUT?

More than four out of five of us routinely flip the lights on to illuminate our path (and perhaps a burglar trodding it) when we're out. Women are more likely than men to remember to flip the switch.

ARE YOU OBSESSIVE?

Relatively few of us suffer from what experts call obsessive compulsive disorder but 48 percent of us claim we regularly double back to make sure that an appliance has been turned off (or on) and that we have out keys. More than half of us who use an alarm clock regularly check it least once to be sure we've set it. Other common causes of worry: whether we've left the iron, oven, coffeepot, car lights, or water on—or forgotten to turn on the burglar alarm or lock the back door.

IS CRIME ON YOUR MIND?

Put it this way: one in four of us has started taking a different route to work to avoid crime.

IS A PENNY SAVED A PENNY EARNED?

Some 11 percent of men and 8 percent of women consider themselves cheapskates. Just 5 percent of those over 45 would admit to such tightfistedness, while 25 percent of so-called Generation Xers share a zeitgeist with Jack Benny.

WHICH STRESSES YOU MORE . . . SPOUSE, BOSS, CO-WORKERS, OR NEIGHBORS?

Don't sell the house. On the stress scale, neighbors are the least offensive causing anxiety for just 23 percent of us—less than parents or shopping. People you have to work with, on the other hand, produce stress for 38 percent of us. Spouses stress us more than our bosses (30 to 26 percent) and the workload has 63 percent of us stressed.

WHAT DO MARKETERS DO THAT DRIVES YOU BATTY?

They employ robots to make aggravating phone calls that always seem to interrupt dinner. This intrusion irks more of us than anything else, followed closely by unsolicited sales calls from humans. Those impossible-to-open childproof caps on medicine bottles get the goat of almost one in five of us and 12 percent are bugged by poor instructions of how to assemble or use products. Seven percent grumble about newspaper ink coming off on our hands.

WHAT WOULD YOU LIKE TO OWN THAT YOU NOW DON'T?

More than a Jacuzzi, hot tub, sauna, or even MTV, we want a pool. Some 23 percent yearn for a backyard swimming hole with men, liberal political thinkers, and families with kids most interested. Maybe it's not the stuff of dreams but 18 percent of us also covet an automatic icemaker and 17 percent a satellite dish.

HAVE YOU EVER SKINNY-DIPPED WITH THE OPPOSITE SEX?

More than one in every four men—28 percent—has taken the plunge in his birthday suit, twice the number of women—14 percent—who've shared a nude swim with the opposite sex.

EVER SUNBATHED NUDE?

We're a prudish lot. Unlike in Europe where it seems half the population hits the sand at the very least topless, in America just under 3 percent of us have bared our butts. Just over 5 percent admit to having gone topless.

EVER HAD A PROFESSIONAL MASSAGE?

Only one in 10 of us has ever paid to be pummeled.

EVER BEEN BUMPED BY AN AIRLINE?

Despite all the talk this topic gets, just 2 percent of us have ever been asked to relinquish a seat on a flight. Many more have missed a plane by getting to the airport late. Amazingly, 28 percent of us have never flown.

WINDOW SEAT OR AISLE?

Overall, we have a vast preference for window seats—though business travelers who fly most often prefer the aisle. Some 57.1 percent of us prefer to nestle in and look out and only 18.1 percent say they regularly request the aisle. Roughly a fourth of us don't care where we sit, as long as we're not cramped between two large people—and the plane gets there safely more or less on time.

WHAT'S IN YOUR GLOVE COMPARTMENT?

Half of us stow maps there. A third also store our insurance cards. Some 23 percent keep a pair of sunglasses. Other often stocked items: writing paper, tissues, and cassette tapes.

DO YOU CONSIDER YOURSELF AN OWL OR A LARK?

The morning people win by a 56 to 44 percent margin. A fourth of those night owls wish they could be early birds.

DO YOU FEEL SAFE?

Ninety-one percent of us feel our neighborhood is safe. More than three out of four—75.4 percent—believe that if we were to scream for help, someone would come to our aid. Amazingly, two-thirds of us feel we have more control over our problems than most characters on TV.

WHAT'S THE HARDEST THING IN THE WORLD TO CONTROL?

Some 38.5 percent of us say the hardest thing in their lives to control is their weight. Another 32.3 percent say they wrestle most with their spending. Just 10.8 percent say the hardest thing to control is their anger, 16.9 percent pinpoint their fears, and 1.5 percent their smoking, drinking, or drug use—or abuse.

OUT OF CONTROL?

Perhaps it has something to do with all those plane crashes but more of us are jittery around an airplane than anywhere else. Forty percent say they feel less secure there than in a car, elevator, home, or workplace—even if it is a U.S. Post Office or fast foodery where shootings have occurred. Slightly more people—27.7 percent—feel out of control in an elevator than they do in a car—26.2 percent.

We feel more in control in our boss's office than in a doctor's examining room or dental chair. But the heart starts beating and adrenaline pumping in a courtroom. A third of us—32.3 percent—register deep discomfort here. Fewer than four out of 10 of us—38.5 percent—feel that if we were falsely accused of a crime, the judicial system would find us innocent. But tipping the scale of out-of-controlness is a visit to the IRS. Almost half of us—43.1 percent—say the prospect makes us weak in the knees.

WOULD YOU RATHER BE ON A DESERTED RURAL ROAD OR INNER CITY STREET CORNER?

Give us the country any time of day. We may buy rap and dress grunge, but give us white picket fence security. Some 43.1 percent of us say we'd feel out in orbit on an inner city street corner—even at noon—while just 4.6 percent would be losing it on a deserted rural road—even at midnight. More than a third of us—36.9 percent—say we'd feel least in control in a country where we didn't speak the language while 13.8 percent would feel out of it at an exclusive and intimidating country club.

WHAT DO YOU DO TO INCREASE YOUR SENSE OF CONTROL?

Almost 5 percent of us own a gun. Six percent have invested in a big fierce looking dog. Fifty-seven percent buy organizer products and almost a third—a devout 29.2 percent—pray. Virtually no one says they imbibe booze or pop tranquility pills—who, then, is taking Prozac?—but 5 percent take their feelings of powerlessness out on someone even less powerful. They dominate subordinates.

DO YOU COMPLAIN?

Seven out of 10 of us never do. We claim we don't know how, or don't think it will help or that companies won't care. Instead, most of us grouse to an average 10 friends or family members about our disappointment. According to the U.S. Office of Consumer Affairs, one out of every four consumer transactions has a glitch.

DO YOU DRESS FOR HALLOWEEN?

Of course kids do. But last year one in five of us so-called grown-ups caught costume fever. More than half—51 percent—put on homemade costumes for All Hallows Eve. Our most popular looks: ghosts, witches, monsters, and entertainment figures compared to animals, especially dinosaurs for kids.

RELATIONSHIPS AND COMMUNIQUÉS

WHERE DO YOU PLACE THE RETURN ADDRESS?

An overwhelming majority of us—91 percent—write our return address on the front left corner of an envelope avoiding the back flap as if it were a uranium mine. Just 7 percent of letter writers put the return address on the back flap and 2 percent do it either way.

HOW DO YOU OPEN THE MAIL?

There is no one way. Two-thirds of us ditch the junk mail unpenetrated. Three out of 10—29 percent—regularly use a letter opener though young ones are three times as likely as older folks to rip and tear. Almost a third of us—31 percent—rip across the top and 22 percent try to neatly tear along the flap. Thirteen percent rip off one end.

DO YOU KEEP A DIARY?

Some 84 percent of us don't keep a diary. Of those few who do, 6 percent write in it daily and 4 percent several times a week. Men are slightly more dedicated daily diarists.

WHAT'S THE FIRST THING YOU DO WHEN YOU COME HOME?

Four times as many men as women hug their spouse first thing when they walk in the door after work. More workers—24 percent—kick off their shoes as the first order of business when they come home than do anything else. Another 20 percent change their clothes while 10 percent listen to their phone messages and 10 percent open the mail. The kids, spouse, and pet get equal priority: 8 percent each hug their offspring, kiss their mate, and attend to their pet first thing. Two percent head straight to the stove. Fewer make a beeline for the computer, TV, or radio.

HOW DO YOU END PERSONAL CALLS?

Four out of 10 of us use the magic words "love you" to sign off.

HOW OFTEN DO YOU CHANGE YOUR ANSWERING MACHINE MESSAGE?

Two out of five don't even have one. Most of us who do are fairly cavalier about these beasts of burden. Once recorded, 46 percent of us rarely or infrequently change the greeting. Less than half of us include our name in the message, with women least likely to do so. A goodly number—76 percent—won't even recite the phone number. (What could they possibly say: "Here's my address, the keys are under the mat?")

DO YOU SEND CHRISTMAS CARDS? HOW MANY?

We are indeed a friendly group. On average we send 38 Christmas cards a year, though married folk, women, and the affluent generally mail more.

WHAT'S THOUGHT FOR FOOD?

More than any other subject at a dinner party, the conversation turns to . . . food: 76 percent of women and 63 percent of men say they've spent time discussing food with another guest at a soiree. Men say they find the major news stories, their jobs and finances, government issues, sports, and what's on tv more chat-worthy. For women, the big topic after food is health, followed by TV shows and the news. Women are considerably likelier than men—52 to 44 percent—to talk about music, family situations—66 to 59 percent—and personal problems—52 to 40 percent.

IF NOT GHOSTBUSTERS, WHO YOU GONNA CALL?

Mom and Dad. Two out of 10 women and one out of 10 men consider their parents their best friends. Almost three out of four—72 percent—would call their parents before anyone else to boast about a child's report card.

WHAT WOULD GET YOU TO CALL THE WHOLE THING OFF?

Three out of four us us say if you can't agree on whether to have kids, don't marry. Just over half of us—52 percent—wouldn't walk down the aisle if he or she and intended weren't compatible in bed. Two out of five of us—44 percent—figure there's trouble ahead if you've got different spending styles. And though James Carville and Mary Matalin among others have demonstrated otherwise, 18 percent feel you need a similar racial, ethnic, religious background and political views for wedded bliss.

HOW DO YOU FEEL ABOUT YOUR MOTHER-IN-LAW?

An astonishing nine out of 10 married women wouldn't mind if she took that proverbial long walk off a short pier. Sociologists say that 90 percent of women feel their husband's mother is the biggest bone of contention in their marriages, ranking right up there with money and sex as the issue to fight about.

WHAT DO YOU AND YOUR SIGNIFICANT OTHER FIGHT ABOUT?

The biggest cause of matrimonial bickering is money. Some 29 percent of couples say they argue more about their spouse's spending habits than anything else. Few consult their mate for routine purchases, but roughly a third say an expenditure above $122 calls for a conference. More than one in five couples—21 percent—keep separate accounts.

The second most hotly contested issue? Whether to watch *Baywatch* or *Seinfeld*. Some 28 percent of couples argue about which TV show to watch followed by 21 percent tiffing about having enough time together, 20 percent about how to discipline the kids, and 16 percent on how the house is kept. Less incendiary are leisure plans: 15 percent go at each other most often about weekend plans, 11 percent on how to spend vacations, and 10 percent on which friends to see. Amazingly, 9 percent say their most vehement riffs concern the proper role of women in society.

DID YOU MARRY YOUR FIRST LOVE?

Two out of five of us who've been married have hooked up with our first love.

HOW OFTEN HAVE YOU FALLEN IN LOVE?

That depends on how old you are. Over the course of a lifetime, six times is normal—starting with puppy love at 13 and the first *serious* relationship four years later. One out of four of us falls in love at least 10 times. Women fall in love more often than men—and end 70 percent of relationships. In a lifetime, 12 percent of us have had at least three unrequited loves.

DID YOU PROPOSE ON BENDED KNEE?

Maybe in the old days that was *de rigeur* but now fewer than one in five of us has proposed—or been proposed to—kneeling. Even less—4 percent—have sought parental approval. Some 6 percent of marriage proposals are made over the phone.

Road Warriors

HOW DO YOU REACT IF ANOTHER DRIVER CUTS YOU OFF?

On the road we're remarkably civil. Cut us off at the pass or in another way get our goat on the highway and 54 percent of men and women *do nothing*. Perhaps this is from passivity, mellowness, or fear of reprisal. The rest of us yell an obscenity (15 percent), give them the finger (7 percent), shake their fists or gesticulate (7 percent), flash their lights (8 percent), or tailgate (3 percent.) Ten percent do something else—presumably pull a gun, cut them off, or turn them in on the car phone.

EVER RUN OUT OF GAS?

Slightly less than half of us (46 percent) have stalled on empty at least once in our lives. Young folks, who are new behind the wheel, tend to run out more than seasoned drivers, and men more than women.

WHEN YOU'RE BEHIND THE WHEEL, WHERE ARE YOUR HANDS?

The traffic department would be appalled to learn that not even half of us drive with both hands on the wheel. (Fifty-five percent of women do; on the other hand, just 35 percent of men drive with both hands on the wheel.) For others—especially young men and the affluent—one hand is out the window, on the gearshift, or fiddling with the radio, car phone, or somesuch. Of those with both mitts on the steering wheel, the most popular position is 10 o'clock and 2 o'clock followed by the 9:00 and 3:00 lineup.

DO YOU APPLY MAKEUP USING THE REARVIEW MIRROR IN YOUR CAR?

Almost three out of four of us occasionally beautify on the go. Of those adding blush in the driver's seat 86 percent say they only do it stopped at lights or in traffic.

WOULD YOU (COULD YOU) CHANGE A TIRE?

You bet. When it comes to road emergencies, we're a fairly self-reliant crew. More than a third of female road warriors would tackle it themselves. More than half would call someone—a friend, a motor club, or garage—or flag someone down. Then there are the desperadoes. No man admitted it, but 6 percent of women drivers confess they'd "look pathetic and hope someone would help."

HOW ABOUT DRIVE A STICK SHIFT?

Almost three of every four of us—71 percent—say they've lurched along driving a car with a manual transmission. Far fewer own them, however.

DO YOU ALWAYS OBEY THE SPEED LIMITS?

Just 45 percent of us claim to consistently tow the speed line. Some 13 percent of 18- to 29-year-old drivers and 1 percent of those over 65 say they *never* obey the speed limit. Almost half of us (42 percent) say we've sailed along at more than 90 miles per hour. The U.S. Federal Highway Administration says three out of five of us put the pedal to the metal with the heaviest concentration of lead foots in Arizona, Rhode Island, Vermont, and New Hampshire and the pokiest in West Virginia, Virginia, Hawaii, and Kentucky.

WHEN DRIVING LATE AT NIGHT DO YOU USUALLY STOP AT STOP SIGNS?

Speed demons we may be, but when it comes to stop signs, the law, we think, is the law. Or maybe it's the fear of a lurking quota-mad policeman but 85.8 percent of us stop. Then again, looked at another way, 14.2 percent don't, with young drivers the most brazen.

DO YOU STOP AT YELLOW TRAFFIC LIGHTS OR SPEED UP AT THEM?

Lead foots, admit it. Two-thirds of Americans see a yellow light and interpret it as last call to the life raft. We zoom through. Northeasterners, surprisingly, are more likely to stop at a yellow traffic light than midwesterners. Women are, less surprisingly, more likely to stop, 30 as opposed to 9 percent.

YOU KNOW YOU SHOULD, BUT DO YOU WEAR YOUR MANUAL LAP BELT?

Assuming, of course, that the contraption doesn't automatically engulf us, a third of us don't buckle up, according to the American Coalition for Traffic Safety. Two-thirds of respondents claim they *always* do, 22 percent sometimes do and 12 percent can't be bothered. Women are more likely to go through the trouble to buckle up than men.

DO YOU FLASH LIGHTS TO WARN ONCOMING TRAFFIC OF A POLICE TRAP AHEAD?

Northeasterners are more than twice as likely as westerners to flash their lights to warn oncoming traffic of a speed trap or other police trap. Almost four out of every 10 people routinely do this courtesy, with singles more thoughtful of their roadmates than marrieds and men more attuned than women.

EVER FOLLOW A COP CAR OR AMBULANCE TO GET THROUGH TRAFFIC FASTER?

One of every five northeasterners would do so in a heartbeat, twice the percentage of westerners or midwesterners. Men also are more than twice as likely as women to ride an ambulance's coattails. Overall, just about one in six of us hitches the through-ride.

WHAT DO YOU DO WHEN YOU AND SOMEONE ELSE REACH THE SAME AVAILABLE PARKING SPOT AT A CROWDED MALL AT THE SAME TIME?

Almost two-thirds of us will fight for it. Only about a quarter of men and a third of all women will graciously relinquish it. Perhaps because in the Northeast where free parking places are at a premium, the citizenry there is more aggressive than elsewhere: 79 percent would rather fight than switch compared to 40 percent of midwesterners.

WHAT ABOUT WHEN YOU'RE CONDENSING INTO A HIGHWAY ENTRANCE RAMP OR TOLL BOOTH?

While midwesterners seem relatively pretty passive when it comes to giving up a parking space, they are more likely to merge with machismo. More than half of men will macho it out, compared to 43 percent of women.

DO YOU ALWAYS LOOK AROUND YOU WHEN PULLING OUT OF A PARKING SPACE?

Virtually everyone looks behind before pulling out—or at least claims to—in order to avoid traffic in the lane they're headed. A very small percentage, basically male, admits they occasionally let the other guy watch out for them.

DO YOU USE YOUR CAR BLINKERS OR THINK THEY'RE THERE FOR COSMETIC PURPOSES?

On the whole, 90 percent of us signal our turns and lane changes. Five percent of women and 12 percent of men don't use their blinkers at all. Midwesterners are just as likely as northeasterners to use them.

DO YOU TAILGATE THINKING YOU CAN MAKE THE CAR AHEAD GO FASTER?

Over a third of us tailgate, 44 percent of men and 30 percent of women. Again, men might need a driver's ed. refresher course. No surprise, the car that's practically in your back seat is probably from the Northeast.

HAVE YOU TRIED TO WHEEDLE OUT OF A TICKET?

Surprisingly, it's not women batting their baby blues to try to get out of a traffic ticket. A third of drivers admit to lying to avoid getting a ticket, but while only one out of four women have done so, more than four out of every 10 men do. Singles and those under 35 are most likely, while upright midwesterners least likely to try.

DO YOU EVER DRIVE AFTER YOU DRINK?

Alarmingly, one driver in four admits to driving after drinking.

DO YOU DO IT IN THE ROAD?

Sing, that is. Contrary to popular belief that we save our arias for the shower or bathroom, most of us find our most appreciative audiences in the car. Almost four of every five of us (78.4 percent) sing in the car—karaoke with the radio—compared to just around half (48.4 percent) who do it in the tub. Another musical spot: the elevator—12.9 get rocking there. And another fourth trill through other bathroom activities. *We* didn't ask which ones.

DO YOU BATHE YOUR CAR REGULARLY?

Just 5 percent of Americans never wash their car. More than one in five of us—22 percent—wash our cars once a week. Eighteen percent wash them every two weeks and another 23 percent figure they wash their vehicles once a month. Nearly half—48 percent—handwash at home, 34 percent claim to use an automatic carwash, and 14 percent use a manual carwash facility.

Sex

ARE YOU GETTING ENOUGH?

Almost a third of men and a quarter of women say they're not having enough sex to sate their appetite. What is enough sex? For most of us, 13 times a month. That's more than twice the actual tally of 6 times a month—and even more than the Sex Information and Education Council's calculation of 57 times a year—or less than 5 times a month. Headaches are no longer the most oft-offered excuse: nowadays, it's plain fatigue.

HOW LONG CAN THIS BE GOING ON?

Counting foreplay—and apparently the whole seduction—as well as the actual act, people say their average sexual experience runs 39 minutes. (They do not say if that also includes the washing up.) With a long-standing partner, the average encounter can take just 16 minutes, and a fourth of the population says their most frequent sessions take 10 minutes or less.

HOW BIG IS YOURS?

Penis, that is. Men say the average length of an erect penis is 10 inches. Women say it's 4 inches. Medical authorities say it falls (or stands) somewhere between at 3 to 4 inches when flaccid and 5 to 7 inches when erect. Almost half of us—46.8 percent—claim size doesn't matter. Unfortunately, for more than half of us, it does.

IF IT DIDN'T HURT OR COST ANYTHING, WOULD YOU HAVE YOUR PENIS OR BREASTS ENLARGED?

A third of men would clamber onto the operating table. Separately, only 5 percent of women say they'd consider breast surgery—5 percent to enlarge their mammaries and 1 percent to make them smaller.

IS PENIS ENVY REAL?

Freud would have us believe that all women are pining away for a penis, but given the choice, only one in five would opt for one.

HAVE YOU EVER DONE IT IN A DANGEROUS PLACE?

What could be more dangerous than at work? While 35 percent of us say it's the bedroom or nothing, 56 percent of men and 42 percent of women say they've had sex at work. One of the more popular rendezvous sites? The boss's office. Perhaps because it's the only one with a sofa.

HAVE YOU EVER HAD AN AFFAIR?

Almost one in three of us has had, or is currently having an extramarital affair—though that doesn't necessarily suggest love. Two-thirds of men and 57 percent of women say they don't love their current lovers. Most women say their lovers are better sex partners than their husbands, while most men prefer their wives better. Almost two-thirds—62 percent—think there's nothing wrong with affairs which typically last almost a year.

HOW ABOUT A ONE-NIGHT STAND?

Sixty percent of men and 54 percent of women at one time in their lives have had at least one one-night stand. One in five men and one in 10 women admit they've had more than a few.

WOMEN, WHEN YOU GIVE ORAL SEX, DO YOU SWALLOW THE SEMEN?

Half never do, and a fourth say they sometimes do. Fewer than one in five say they actually enjoy doing so.

WHAT'S YOUR FANTASY?

We may not like to swallow, but oral sex makes good fantasy fodder. We daydream about that more than anything else, followed by doing it with a famous person or many partners. A third of women are absolute clams about their sexual preferences.

WHICH DO YOU PREFER, THE PRELUDE—OR THE ORCHESTRA?

If we had to choose between hugging but no sex or sex but no hugging, two-thirds would choose the former. But that's not really the question, is it? Two-thirds of us prefer "the act" itself to foreplay—with men (73 to 58 percent) likelier tham women to feel this way.

HOW OFTEN DO YOU TAKE MATTERS INTO YOUR OWN HANDS?

At least you presumably are having sex with someone you like. More than twice as many men as women confess they masturbate, and singles twice as often as marrieds. Most 18- to 40-year-old men say they masturbate at least two times a week and mostly—though not exclusively—at home. Most women the same age say they do it roughly once a week.

SURE IT'S TIGHT AND TICKLISH TO GET ON, BUT DO YOU WEAR ONE?

Fewer than a third of men use condoms regularly. But three out of five insist on them on a first sex date. Amazingly, 16 percent of people say that at least once they haven't used one—when they thought there was a possibility of contracting

AIDS. Women buy 4 out of 10 of all the condoms sold. Fewer than 20 percent of sexually active people choose them as their first choice for birth control. Most pick sterilization—but that's permanent, and many relationships are not.

WHAT'S YOUR SPERM COUNT?

It may be as much a badge of manhood as your total net worth (and far higher) though few of us could rattle the digits off. During orgasm, the normal guy emits 120 million to 600 million sperm in his teaspoon of ejaculate. (Only about 400 of them will get anywhere *near* the egg.) More evidence that men today aren't cut out of John Wayne cloth: since 1940, the average male's sperm count has dropped 42 percent from 113 million per millilter to 66 million. Eighteen-year-olds have on average 30 percent more sperm than 45-year-olds.

HAVE YOU BEEN TESTED FOR AIDS?

The National Center for Health Statistics says just 15 percent of sexually active adults have been tested for the HIV virus—but our informal survey shows almost three times that. Not surprisingly, more men have taken the test than women, but the gap is narrowing. Interestingly, fewer than one in 10 of us has been tested for syphilis or gonorrhea.

HOW KINKY ARE YOU?

Someone is buying all those whips and chains. Five percent of us claim we're into bondage and 8 percent regularly perform anal sex. Almost one in five of us—18 percent—regularly use pornographic material to spice up the sex act and more than one in 10—11 percent—use some sort of sexual device—vibrators, electric toothbrushes, you name it. Some 58 percent say dirty talk is part of the fun. Despite the loudness of the Moral Majority's cry, more than one in five of us—22 percent—have rented a porn flick at least once.

WILL YOU DO IT PROM NIGHT?

Forget the corsage—bring Kama Sutra. Almost half of all teens—45 percent—expect to go all the way on prom night. More than one in four—28 percent—plan to do it at a rented hotel room, 23 percent aim to cozy up in the back of the car, and 4 percent to go to a friend's house.

DOES ROVER WATCH?

If only Fido could speak, what an X-rated movie director he could be. Of the half of us who have animals at home—not counting our sex partners, almost half—45.4 percent—allow our pets in the room during sex. Repressed midwesterners are least likely to allow Cleo or Duke in as observers.

SHOPPING

WHO IS TAKING THE FIRST MILK IN THE DAIRY CASE?

Amazingly, almost three of every four of us reach behind the front milk in the freezer case to take a fresher carton. Midwesterners are least likely to do so, but even they pay attention to freshness dating. In fact, while only eight out of 10 of us read labels religiously, 95 percent regularly check out "best if used by" dates.

WHEN YOU DON'T WANT SOMETHING IN YOUR SHOPPING CART, WHAT DO YOU DO WITH IT?

Assuming it's not perishable like a pint of Häagen Dazs coffee ice cream, almost half of us—45.2 percent—leave the spurned item in another part of the store where we happen to be when we realized we don't want the bag of pork rinds light. Southerners are the laziest: 53.7 of them ditch the unwanted goods wherever they are—and justify it perhaps by supplying employment for high school students who must restack them. An additional 5.2 percent (with younguns 10 times likelier than older folks) conceal the crime, hiding the unwanted food behind something else. A third of us—32.9 percent—bring it back to its rightful place and 8.4 percent ask a stock clerk to replace it. Another 5.8 percent leave it at the checkout line.

DO YOU SNACK ON THE STORE'S FOOD WHILE YOU SHOP?

Perhaps because women still spend more time in the supermarket than men, they're more prone to nibble on the store's merchandise—uninvited. Around one of every four of us—21.9 percent—plops a grape or two; loose candies and nuts in the bulk food section are similarly vulnerable. So are cookies in the bake shop. Despite many salad bar signs warning that sampling is unsanitary or against the law, about 20 percent do it, with young people three times as likely as older ones.

DO YOU TAKE THE FREE SAMPLES OFFERED?

It's a different story when the store offers the samples. Three of every five of us take the freebie demonstration foods served up in the supermarket. Of those, on average, 37 percent wind up purchasing what we've sampled.

DO YOU READ THE MAGS WHILE WAITING ON THE CHECKOUT LINE—AND NOT BUY THEM?

How do you imagine the *National Enquirer, Soap Opera Digest, Vogue et. al.* got so dog-earred? More than half of us shoppers figure that if the line is long, a little free reading is our due. Some 51.9 percent of us read a magazine while standing in line and then put it back without buying. (It's also why when we do buy, three-fourths of us will reach behind or under for a fresher copy.) Yet 22 percent of shoppers consider reading without buying bad form. Six percent huff that they'd never shop at a store where they'd have to wait so long. Women and northeasterners are likelier than anyone to peek in the pages—perhaps because the checkout lines are longest and their patience shortest.

DO YOU TAKE LIBERTIES IN THE EXPRESS LINE?

Aren't you the one who always manages to wheel in right behind the cheater? More than one in every four of us tries to take the shorter express line with more items than the maximum posted. Some 27.4 percent of us—more women than men and roughly twice the share of northeasterners to mid-westerners—sneak more items than we should on to the conveyer. Most justify it because they're adding only two items but almost 10 percent try to slip by five or more items above the posted limit.

DO YOU SHOP ON IMPULSE?

More than three-fourths of us—77 percent—head to the supermarket with a list. Yet 52.6 percent of all supermarket merchandise is bought on impulse. Goods flanking the cashier are the most frequently purchased "impulse items."

DO YOU LEAVE YOUR XMAS SHOPPING TO THE LAST MINUTE?

Twenty-two percent of men and 9 percent of women leave it for the day or two before. Twelve percent of us start out with the January sales and a fifth of us anticipatory folks begin in the summer or fall before. But for fully half of us Thanksgiving fires the gun for the start of the holiday shopping season.

DO YOU WEAR PEDS WHEN TRYING ON SHOES?

More than three out of five of us (61.4 percent) try on a shoe with a covered foot. Oddly, only half all of midwesterners do.

DO YOU ALWAYS TRY CLOTHES ON IN THE DRESSING ROOM?

While most of us head to the fitting rooms, more than a fourth of us occasionally improvise by trying clothes on in the aisles, slipping them over what we're wearing.

DOES BUYING SOMETHING NEW MAKE YOU HAPPY?

It does the trick for almost three out of four of us—73 percent—but much more for women than men—81 versus 64 percent—and for younger folks more so than their elders. Some 92 percent of 18- to 24-year-olds say making a purchase gives them a lift—whereas only 57 percent of 25- to 34-year-olds get the glow. For two-thirds of us—65 percent—the store is a celebration destination. Just one in five women heads to the stores when she's feeling low.

ARE YOU MALL MAD?

Most of us dip into a department store 16.1 times a year, while so-called fashion statements pop in 22.8 times. The "normal" shopper spends 4 hours a month at a mall—compared to 7 or 8 hours a decade ago. On a typical visit *she* spends 55 minutes—and $34.

HOW DO YOU FEEL ABOUT SHOPPING?

Just 7 percent of Americans don't like to shop and try to avoid it. Another 36 percent do it somewhat grudgingly—they get what they need and leave. Another 11 percent say that while it's not their first choice for fun, they don't mind shopping once they're in the store. A third of Americans are mildly enthusiastic—enjoying shopping and yearning for more time and money.

In ZZZZZ Land

We spend an average seven and a half hours in dreamland—the same amount of time as we spend working. In a lifetime, it comes to 220,000 hours or approximately a third of our lives. Considerable, but not as bad as cats who doze away 15 hours a day.

Roughly two-thirds of us consider sleep a necessity more than a pastime. If there were a pill that would refresh and restore us the way sleep does, most of us would gladly pop it, leaving more time for sex, TV, partying, and work.

WHAT'S YOUR SLEEP POSITION?

Just about the same number of people sleep on the left side as on their right—34.2 percent each. A fourth of us sleep on our stomach and 14 percent on our back. Age, money, whether we're married or not, and where we live don't make a difference. The only thing that might affect our sleep position is whether we do it alone. Almost 70 percent start off spooning—that is, nestled together—and then as we settle in, separate.

WHAT KIND OF BED DO YOU LIKE?

Two-thirds of us prefer firm to soft, but roughly four of every 10 of us—41 percent—think a standard double bed is the ideal size. A third prefer queen and one out of five finds waving to their partners across a king-sized bed hunky-dory. The Lucille Ball–Desi Arnez setup rings a bell for a small number of us. Six percent *prefer* twin beds. Another 3 percent won't say.

DO YOU STEAL THE COVERS . . . OR HAVE THEM STOLEN OUT FROM OVER YOU?

Three-fourths of both men and women accuse their partners of hogging the covers. Perhaps what the world needs is a retracting ruler–type mechanism that governs the amount of blanket each partner can snatch and protects the victim.

EVEN IN HOT WEATHER, DO YOU USE A BLANKET?

It seems most Americans aren't using a cover for warmth. More than four out of five women (83 percent) use a cover for weight or security, while six out of 10 men do. Women, more than men, tend to wrap up in the blanket while one in five of us admits to letting a leg dangle out.

HOW DO YOU LIKE THE ROOM TEMP?

Chilly. But though a vast majority of us prefer a cool room to a warm one, hot-blooded men often like it so cold penguins can breed in the bedroom. One woman pined for a climate zone modulator that would let the left side of the bed bask in 70 degree warmth while the right frosts over.

WHO GOES TO BED FIRST?

For most couples, more often then not, it's lights out at the same time. More than 60 percent of marrieds and live-togethers prefer to go to bed at the same time as their mate. But responsibilities (like who has to get up first) and fatigue usher one or the other into dreamland first.

EVER SLEPT APART FROM YOUR MATE OVER A SPAT?

The spare bedroom couch gets some workout. More than a third of women—36 percent—have at least once slept apart from their husband because of a fight.

WHAT DO YOU SLEEP IN?

Some 23 percent of us claim to wear nightgowns to bed—including 2 percent of men. Fewer sleep in pajamas, T-shirts, or underwear. For 15 percent, nothing comes between them and their sheets—though three times as many rich people as poor sleep nude. (Perhaps they got rich by not spending money on clothes no one sees.) Just 6 percent of women sleep nude and only 2 percent in their underwear.

Just about four out of every 10 of us sleep with some jewelry on—with women 16 percent more likely than men to do so and inexplicably, left-handeds more likely than anyone.

DO YOU LOCK YOUR BEDROOM DOOR WHEN YOU GO TO SLEEP?

Now we're talking about keeping out another sort of intruder—and 26.4 percent of us would do so. Some 8.7 percent of us lock the door routinely with southerners almost three times as likely as westerners to do so. Three out of four married people never lock the bedroom door. Marrieds with children seem least likely to lock their doors.

DO YOU LET SLEEPING DOGS LIE . . . WITH YOU, THAT IS?

Just under half (48 percent) of all dog owners welcome Rover into the sheets—or at least the foot of the bed, though they claim they hate the bouncing. For most he's banished to the floor. Cats decide where they sleep—but when they hop aboard owners say that the grooming that goes on can drive them bonkers.

WHO SLEEPS BETTER?

Men do. Women typically have shorter periods of deep sleep than their men. That's because the men are likelier to snore, jar the bed, and cause a trough in the mattress, forcing them to sleep on an incline, according to the Better Sleep Council. Men sleep slightly more and insomnia is more common in women. The average person wakes up ever so briefly 15 times night—without ever being aware of it. On any given night, a third of us are tossing and turning. Just 25 percent of us say we always get a restful night's sleep.

EVER TAKE SLEEPING PILLS?

If Tylenol PM and Benadryl count, then 86 percent of America has at one time or another tried more than hot milk and counting sheep.

DO YOU SNORE?

Some 27 percent of the population saws wood with 36 percent of men and 23 percent of women guilty of disturbing the peace. But for the over 60 crowd, the percentage soars. Six out of 10 older men snore. After menopause women start to catch up with men.

DO YOU SLEEPWALK?

Not likely. Just one in 40 adult men and women sleepwalks occasionally. And one in six children between ages 5–12 sleepwalks at least once. One in eight of us suffers from nightmares. Men are more likely to sleepwalk than women and young children, likelier than adolescents.

DO YOU GET THIRSTY AT NIGHT?

More than a third of us (36.1 percent) keep a glass of water or other drink by the bedside at night.

HOW MANY PILLOWS DO YOU USUALLY SLEEP WITH?

Roughly one of every six northeasterners sleep virtually sitting up—propped up by four or more pillows. Their numbers 15.4 percent are more than double the national average. More than half of all westerners, on the other hand, prefer one or no pillow. Most of us use two (42.6 percent) or one (37.1 percent). More than 10 percent use three pillows and 3.2 percent sleep with none at all.

ARE YOUR PILLOWS ON TOP OF THE BEDSPREAD OR NESTLED UNDERNEATH?

Roughly seven out of 10 of us show our pillows to the world, with midwesterners more likely to let them hang out. The rest tuck them under—or vary the display depending on whether company's coming.

DO YOU SLEEP WITH A STUFFED ANIMAL?

Don't short the stock of companies that sell teddy bears. One in five grown women confesses to sleeping regularly with a stuffed animal—that is presumably not her mate. Five percent of grown men also admit it. The under 35 set and unmarrieds seem most in need of nurturing.

HOW ABOUT WITH THE LIGHT ON?

Three percent of us can't get to dreamland in the dark. We leave on a night-light or a light in the hall. And even 16 percent of the 97 percent of us who sleep with the bedroom light off when we're in our own beds turn shaky on the road, devising filtered light systems from the bathroom to illuminate unfamiliar terrain.

DO YOU FALL ASLEEP WITH THE TV OR RADIO ON?

For more than one of every five of us the news is better than a sleeping pill. Some 21.6 percent of us fall asleep clutching the remote control all the time—and 54.8 percent do it sometimes. Southerners and northeasterners are far more likely than westerners to do so. Just 15.2 percent of the overall population says they never do.

ANSWERS TO THE NORMALCY TEST

SEE HOW YOU COMPARE WITH OTHERS:

1. Seventy-three percent reach behind for a fresher carton, 85 percent of men go over the top of their undies, 58.4 percent eat corn methodically, 91 percent put their address on the top left corner, 48 percent drive with both hands on the wheel, and 42 percent squeeze the toothpaste from the middle.

2. Almost half of us—45.2 percent—leave it where we are, 5.2 percent hide it, 32.9 percent bring it back to its rightful place, 8.4 percent ask a stock clerk to replace it, and 5.8 percent leave it at the checkout line.

3. Just over 6 percent of us run the Chivas under the tap, while 10 percent empties the cheaper private label stuff into the more status-plus brand container. Thirteen percent of us occasionally do our offspring's homework, 16 percent try to influence doc but 76 percent wouldn't dream of compromising him, and 60 percent are likely to sneak out the Scotch tape.

4. Some 29 percent use letter openers, 31 percent rip across the top, 22 percent neatly tear along the flap, 13 percent rip one end off.

5. Some 69 percent eat cake first, 28 percent eat the frosting, and 3 percent eat them together.

6. Half eat Oreos whole, 18 percent twist them apart, and 15 percent dunk them. Some 19 percent add them to something or smash them.

7. Some 49 percent put on their panties first, and a third add the bra while 16 percent put on their hose next, 19 percent start with the bra, 15 percent wear our hose *under* our panties, and 22 percent can't recall

8. Three and two-fifths percent sleep with none, 37.1 percent with one, 42.6 percent with two, 10 percent with three, and 7 percent with four or more.

9. Fifty-three percent pull the toilet paper from over the top, 46.5 percent of men say they always put the seat down after they pee, 32 percent would *never* sit on a public throne and 12.3 percent wouldn't give it a second thought, and 25 percent prefer the handicapped stall because it's roomier. Sixteen percent run water to camouflage tinkle.

10. Just 2 percent have been bumped, 46 percent have run out of gas, 28 percent of men and 14 percent of women have taken the plunge in their birthday suits, under 3 percent of us have bared our butts, and 40 percent have paid to be pummeled.

11. Some 57.1 percent prefer to look out versus 18.1 percent who ask for the aisle, 45 percent keep both hands on the wheel when they drive, 66 percent zoom through yellows, 40 percent claim to floss but fewer really do, 20 percent bite nails, and 11 percent usually pick off their scabs.

12. Fifty-four percent do nothing, 15 percent yell an obscenity, 7 percent give them the finger, 7 percent shake their

fists or gesticulate, 8 percent flash their lights, 3 percent tailgate and 10 percent do something else.

13. Forty-seven percent brush them up and down, 25 percent do it in a fastidious circular motion, 15 percent do side to side, 7 percent angle it, 2 percent use an electric brush, and 1 percent soak.

14. Eighteen percent can cross our eyes, 32 percent can flare their nostrils, 68 percent can snap their fingers, 22.9 percent of men and 6.5 percent of women can whistle loudly, 67 percent can roll their tongues, 13.2 percent can wiggle their ears, 30 percent can raise an eyebrow at a time, 40 percent of men and 10 percent of women can juggle, and 18 percent can do a split.

15. Forty-six percent tap or jiggle their knees or legs, 44.5 percent chew on ice, 40 percent crack their knuckles, 27.1 percent regularly chew a pen cap or pencil, 38 percent peel the labels off bottles or cans, 30 percent twist or pull on their hair, 26.1 percent twist the phone cord, and 20 percent grind their teeth.

16. Some 34.2 percent never send food back to the kitchen, 22.6 percent take home doggybags, 42 percent would consider withholding a tip for rotten service, 65 percent would summon the courage to ask to change tables, while 28.3 percent would not address the issue.

17. Thirty-two percent keep their watches at real time, 34 percent set it ahead five minutes, 8 percent set it ahead 10 minutes, 16 percent of us move it ahead—but aren't sure by how much. Four percent don't wear a watch.

18. Almost twenty-eight percent skip ahead to find out what's going to happen, 43.5 percent always finish a book once they start it, and 42.9 percent occasionally use the page itself as a bookmark.

19. Seventy-nine percent don't make their bed every day, 13 percent alphabetizes books and records, 49 percent are likely to slip on the latex gloves.

20. Forty-four percent smooth out the tinfoil, 57 percent reuse giftwrap, 66 percent amass rubber bands, 54 percent occasionally pass along an unwanted gift, and 52 percent have stashes of old pennies.